The Psychology of Sport

The Psychology of Sport: Facing One's True Opponent

by
Robert W. Grant

McFarland & Company, Inc., Publishers
Jefferson, North Carolina, and London

Library of Congress Cataloguing-in-Publication Data

Grant, Robert W., 1952–
 The psychology of sport.

 Bibliography: p. 163.
 Includes index.
 1. Sports — Psychological aspects. I. Title.
GV706.4.G73   1988   796′.01   87-43197

ISBN 0-89950-271-7 (acid-free natural paper)

Printed in the United States of America.

McFarland & Company, Inc., Publishers
 Box 611, Jefferson, North Carolina 28640

This book is dedicated to my parents.

To my father for instilling in me his love of athletics and for always keeping this world in perspective.

To my mother for imparting to me her insight into the beauty and absurdity of competitive athletics.

Without their influence I would still be caught in the mire and have been unable to compose this book, which is written in the hope of sparing many the tragedy of failing unnecessarily and the lifelong feeling of confusion and shame they may bear for not realizing their dreams, despite their own best efforts.

Table of Contents

Preface

Each person picking up this book must be asking, Does this book apply to me? Is it relevant for coaches? The answers to the above questions are that this book is designed for anyone, regardless of age or gender, who is involved in sports, whether as participant, supervisor or spectator. It is invaluable to anyone who supervises an athlete's career or personal life. This applies to coaches and parents in particular.

This book is also directed at the athlete. It will introduce and expand his or her awareness of the tremendously important role that the mind plays in all dimensions of athletic performance. An individual's degree of athletic success will be, in most cases, in direct proportion to his or her mental stability and awareness of the reasons for starting and continuing to compete.

As we shall see, most athletes are unaware of what drives them in relation to their sport. Not being aware of motives, which typically have a long developmental history, is the primary reason athletes "choke" — not only in actual competition but also in the choice of team and coach and, most specifically, in the design of training routines.

The main thesis of this book is that most athletes defeat

themselves, for a variety of psychological and emotional reasons, the majority of which are unconscious. The superior athlete is not always the one who is most physically gifted but frequently is the most self-assured and self-aware.

What distinguishes an average from an exceptional athlete cannot be stated as just physical skills and endowments. It is the attitude and strength of one's mind under pressure that make the difference.

The level and quality of an athlete's performance in competition are frequently used to assess how appropriate and successful his or her training and preparation have been. To understand what contributes to superior performance the focus needs to be far broader. The constitution of an athlete's personality and style of performing have been cast long before the playing field. It is especially in regard to the developmental unfolding of their personalities that athletes need to do homework, for it is this that dictates how they handle the physical, technical and emotional demands of their sport.

All athletes must become aware of how their approaches to the sport evolved and the reasons behind these highly individualistic developments. The quality of the athlete's capacity to perform will be a function of his or her ability to appropriately respond to a myriad of external and internal phenomena. This ability lies at the core of the athlete's chances for success and it is this ability that will be the primary focus of this work.

Every spectator and athlete wants to know how some competitors are able to develop certain intangible qualities like "hustle," "desire," and "killer instinct," and what it is about others who "won't quit" and are cool under pressure. Most people are confused as to whether these qualities are innate or learned. Are they the result of a driven athlete who is terrified of failure or the byproducts of a mentally stable and well integrated individual? This work will answer these questions and show why so many physically gifted athletes are unable to develop the aforementioned characteristics. In short, this book will dissect the mental and emotional components of sports performance.

This work will be directed towards female as well as male athletes. Women must confront many of the same issues that their male counterparts do. But in addition they must also deal with issues related to body image, gender identity and male stereotypes about what is proper feminine behavior, as they continue to enter sports that have traditionally been dominated by males.

The issues for women may be different in regard to specifics, but their task is the same as that of men: to become strong enough psychologically and emotionally that they can develop their inherent physical and technical abilities to the maximum. This book will demonstrate why this is not such an easy task. There are many personal, cultural and societal factors that impede an athlete's attempts to actualize his or her talents.

There is no doubt that most future breakthroughs in athletic performance will take place in the mental arena. It is the new frontier of athletic research. As body-building equipment and technical improvements in paraphernalia reach their limits, it is the mental component of performance that will be focused upon and will provide enormous rewards for those willing to venture into it. Many, if not all, major performance improvements in the next ten years will come from the mental side. This will include issues relating to motivation, lapses in confidence (slumps), performance anxiety, failures to rehabilitate after injuries, problems in interpersonal relations and communication (between players, coaches and administrators), and placement of athletes in the proper sport and with teams and coaches that have compatible philosophies and styles.

Introduction

This book proposes a new slant on sports psychology, which has traditionally focused on such issues as the personality traits typically found in successful athletes. Sports psychology has also provided athletes with relaxation techniques so they can be more at ease and attuned to the demands of their athletic task. Similarly, sports psychologists have supplied athletes with exercises in guided imagery. Through certain mental exercises or rehearsals the athlete is able to mentally visualize completing a specific athletic event or act in perfect form. For example, a pole vaulter imagines every step leading up to and including a perfect vault. It is believed that such "trial runs" enhance actual performance by programming the body to perfection through exact and successful mental enactments. Hypnosis is also frequently used to help the athlete remove unconscious mental blocks that inhibit maximal performance.

Traditional sports-psychology praxis renders valuable benefits but at the same time is limited in its ability to comprehend the whole gamut of psychological pressures and demands involved in athletic performance.

Several important dimensions of the athlete's mentality will be

1

exposed and analyzed in order to understand how an athlete's mind either facilitates or obstructs athletic performance. This book is intended to reveal how an athlete's upbringing, athletic history, personality (with its strengths and weaknesses), and personal interactions with coaches and others all come together to produce the athlete's unique style of performing and handling pressure on and off the playing field.

To be a top-flight athlete, an individual must have certain physical strengths and skills. To what degree an athlete possesses these characteristics is debatable. For example, an athlete who weighs at least 190 pounds and is able to do a 4.3 forty-yard sprint fits the professional profile of a pro running back. Everyone knows, however, that having these physical capabilities is no guarantee of success. There are too many other intangible factors involved. The physical dimension, as every athlete knows, is not enough, except in extraordinary cases. The sophistication of top-flight athletics and the plenitude of superior performers have brought an end to the days of the dumb and emotionally unstable jock.

The reader will have several concerns when reading this book. For instance, What is sports psychology and how does it differ from traditional coaching practices and contemporary psychological theories and practices? Compared to traditional coaching, sports psychology, while paying attention to an athlete's physical endowments and technical proficiencies, focuses on these dimensions only as they are lived out and expressed by the athlete, or, to put it a different way, as they exemplify the athlete's sense of identity and mental approach to sport. A typical question a sports psychologist might ask in this regard is, Why has the athlete overdeveloped certain aspects of his sport (a miler, his stamina for instance) and left underdeveloped other dimensions (sprinting ability, say)? A basketball player's failure to develop rebounding and defensive skills, while overdeveloping an offensive shot repertoire, says much about the athlete's personality, mental blocks, ego needs, fears, and so forth.

The sports psychologist must ask how such a style evolved — what its developmental history is, and how this attitude or stylistic approach to the game of basketball can enhance, or more typically impede, the athlete's chances of success. For example, a gifted soccer player with tremendous one-on-one offensive skills will encounter severe obstacles when working for a coach who has a "team concept" approach to the game. Stan Terliki and Drago Drumbovic of the Pittsburgh Spirit professional soccer team are excellent examples of this type of athlete. Such a player will obviously be looked at in terms of his strengths and weaknesses. He will receive some playing time in respect to the former, and his total playing time will be determined by other factors. Terliki's and Drumbovic's style, for the most part, was opposed to their coach's philosophy.

On the Spirit team, a well-rounded player's marketability and opportunities for playing time are increased, and these enhance his or her chances for success and for maintaining a high level of confidence. The issue that a sports psychologist needs to understand is why athletes are so invested in a particular style that they cannot compromise or adapt to the coach's "team approach." What prevents athletes from developing a less egotistical approach to their sport in view of the fact that failure to modify style will most likely not only damage their careers, but more crucially their capability to perform on a day-to-day basis? As it turned out, Drumbovic was traded in 1984 and Terliki was auctioned off in 1985.

A sports psychologist will want to ask how the athlete's mindframe affects performance under the stress and challenge of topflight competition. Does the athlete excel or choke under pressure? Some athletes give their best performances under pressure. The sports psychologist needs to understand how emotionally rattled athletes handle the pressures of a particular situation such that they cannot perform anywhere near their peak.

The sports psychologist recognizes and affirms the importance of coaching, practice, the development of conditioning and technique. These, without a doubt, are essential to athletic success, but are not *sufficient*. How the athlete reacts to coaching directives, utilizes practice sessions, and develops personal conditioning and technique is much more important. Just how the athlete's state of mind either facilitates or impedes maximum preparation and performance is the true focus of the sports psychologist.

The physical and mental aspects of the athlete are both crucial to the overall level of achievement. Traditionally, too much emphasis has been put on the physical and not enough on the mental.

When coaches attempt to motivate athletes through pep talks, personal attention, special drills to develop the weak parts of their game, or through "head games" (being strict, intimidating, easygoing, fatherly, and so forth), they come near and often realize the importance of the psychological domain. Yet unless coaches are extremely sensitive their attempts to work on the mind of the athlete are often too general and regimented. They do not take into consideration the unique personality and history of each athlete. Coaches have historically had an unwritten rule to stay out of athletes' personal lives. Their function was to drive their athletes like "real men," not to hold their hands in a maternal way.

The other side of the coin is that athletes typically have to fit the coach's preconceived ideas of how they should take up their sport. Some can adapt to the coach's regime and therefore fit in. Many, however, cling to their preferred ways of performing because their fragile egos prevent compromise. They either play poorly or not at all when their style is contradictory to their coach's. This situation is the rule in competitive athletics in the United States. Very often, an athlete's career either plateaus or ends because of an inability to adapt to a coach's personality and philosophy of the game. If a young athlete stumbles or falls, he or she can usually be replaced, especially at the highest levels of competition. Many careers end prematurely because of athletes' inability to have productive relationships with their coaches. Every inner-city neighborhood is filled with athletes of the highest caliber who are casualties in the game of human relationships. This is a tragedy, the effects of which often last a lifetime.

The early demise of a potentially brilliant career leaves an athlete with an indelible sense of failure and inadequacy. These feelings may haunt the individual the rest of his or her life. Saddest, perhaps, is that the athlete has little insight into the fact that failure was mainly due to mental instability and immaturity. The athlete's sense of self, with its fears and emotional scars, typically and unconsciously sabotages personal attempts at self-improvement and success. Athletes themselves, for the most part, limit or destroy their athletic careers and the possibility of actualizing their potential.

There are many reasons why so many physically gifted and intelligent athletes fail or disappear into oblivion. Any top-flight athlete will tell you that there is much more to athletic excellence than just physical skills. Diet, sleep, and intimate personal relationships have a tremendous effect on performance. All of these aspects affect the athlete's physical health and emotional well-being, but very little attention is given to their relationship and the athlete's capacity to perform. An athlete's sense of emotional well-being is the soil out of which physical skills blossom.

Most coaches are aware, to different degrees, that athletes' overall sense of mental health and clear understanding of their motives will greatly influence not only their immediate performance but their career. Traditionally (but with several notable exceptions) this has not been the explicit focus of coaches. Theirs is a world of strategy, conditioning, training, technique, and ploys designed to prepare their athletes to psych out their opponents. This speaks, at least minimally, to a coach's awareness of just how influential the mind is in athletic performance. Unfortunately, the most effective psyching out done by coaches has often been in regard to themselves and their own players.

Within the arena of sports, traditional psychology can be set free from many of its self-imposed limitations. In fact, most sports psychologists are extremely conservative in their approach to athletes.

Sports psychology, as defined in this work, differs from traditional psychology in several regards. Sports psychology deals with athletes' styles of performing, how they integrate their sports into the rest of their lives and how athletic accomplishments speak to their overall sense of self. The aim is to maximize the athlete's sense of "sports self"—the conscious awareness of what is driving him or her to concentrate so much in a particular sport.

Athletes' accomplishments will be in direct proportion to their overall emotional and psychological maturity. Sports and depth psychology become much more akin at this point. By focusing on the sport component of an athlete's identity we touch upon many, if not all, of the athlete's personal qualities and history. These latter dimensions are part of the athlete's mentality, which is made up of personal life choices and circumstances. Athletics is the explicit focus of the sports psychologist, whose ultimate goal is to engender emotional awareness and stability so that the athlete can maximize individual athletic potential.

Sports psychologists have not allowed themselves to go into the prime areas of athletic expression. There is very little in the literature by any psychologist that deals with an athlete's psychological and developmental history and the psychological components of athletic performance. To help the athlete professionally, one must know how he or she trains and performs and the underlying reasons.

The way an athlete practices and performs says much about the nature of his or her reality and identity. Knowing how the family pressured, encouraged, or discouraged the child athletically can aid in understanding the current status of the athlete's capability to perform. A sports psychologist must see concretely how these historical and present psychic influences contribute to the athlete's daily training format and way of performing.

Contemporary psychology is unfamiliar with the athlete as a person enmeshed in a complex of motivational influences and personal relationships. The athlete is not just a body or a machine involved in a sport, although he or she is often treated as such. The athlete is a person who performs in accordance with the meaning an athletic endeavor has in his life, and how it contributes to the athlete's sense of personal worth in relation to all those people who affect him. These people, whether dead or alive, affect the specific way an athlete takes up the quest for excellence and self-fulfillment or fails to. A sports psychologist *must* be attuned to these dynamics.

Sports psychology is one concrete expression of psychology's overall intention to help individuals free themselves from personal conflicts and fears, thus helping them reach their full potential. This book will demonstrate that athletic and personal development are not mutually exclusive, but must occur simultaneously, in a proper balance, and emerge out of the same ground for an athlete to be capable of excelling.

As opposed to contemporary psychology, sports psychology focuses on the "athletic self" of the individual. Such a focus is exciting and upbeat; it deals with the positive and the affirmative side of life. Athletes are typically highly motivated. They are, typically, high-energy and positive people who want to develop themselves to the maximum. They are always looking at some dimension of their life, and want to analyze and develop themselves in order to get the edge on their competitors.

Life can be very difficult, especially if we grow up without material advantages or a stable and warm home life. Most people, even the fortunate ones, have their hands full just trying to cope with the complexities of life. Yet there are those who are gifted, and have a strong will to excel. These people want more out of life than just getting by or surviving. They may want to create something personal — something that goes beyond the mundane. Such individuals want to put their personal stamp on reality, and more specifically, their sport. They are the pathfinders, the creators, the geniuses. They inspire us to attempt and eventually accomplish what is normally considered impossible. It is this type of athlete who will always be in the background of this work, for this person exists in all of us. We just need the courage and insight to call that person forth and draw from his or her strength.

This work will begin with a look at the developmental unfolding of an athlete's sports identity and career. The focus will be on the constantly changing emotional and psychological environment that a developing athlete must encounter. It is these environments, or microcosms, that form the individual's sense of self and the motives for wanting to be an athlete. All the major psychological influences that bombard an athlete's life from infancy to adulthood will be tracked. We will begin with a look at the sports environment of the home. It is here that a "sports world" exists even prior to the birth of the potential athlete. This world of sportive expectations gets the ball rolling for an infant's budding life and athletic career. Later chapters will elaborate on how these early influences get played out in all aspects of the individual's athletic career.

The central thesis of this book is that no matter how gifted an athlete is physically, he or she is not going to improve or perform anywhere near full potential if unmotivated, or confused or ambivalent. In such a case, the athlete most likely will end up as a failure, or feel like one.

1
Family History

Every child is born into a family that has feelings about athletics, whether pro or con. Parents and siblings set up an environment of values and expectations in which a would-be child athlete must navigate. Children must steer this course in order to win their parents' approval, thereby insuring that their emotional and physical needs will be met. Even before birth, there exists a world of athletic expectations, lost dreams, and insecurities that the child's parents and siblings have lived through. This is primarily made up of the parents' attitudes towards athletics, which are derived from the relative success of their own athletic careers.

Every child's task from birth is to grow and develop — at a minimum, to survive. The best way to do this is to form a strong bond with its parents, one based on mutual love and appreciation. Through this bond, the child hopes to receive the necessary love, attention, and energy it needs to develop. The way many children's needs are met, unfortunately, is by conforming to the parents' expectations, no matter how bizarre or unrealistic they may be.

As the child begins to mature and develop muscular coordination, the urgency of the parents' athletic aspirations for him becomes more pronounced. Some children receive a great deal of pressure very early to perform at a level beyond their current development. Some parents irrationally feel that their child *must* have interest and proficiency for certain highly valued sports, those the parents, for many reasons, are highly invested in. The child's slow progress or lack of interest may result in serious disappointment for the parents and cause them to withdraw affection, and most destructively, approval.

Take swimming, for example. Some swimmers start training (competitive or otherwise) as early as three years of age. Some parents have even started their child at three months of age, and not just to "pool safe" him or her because of accessibility to a swimming pool. They want their child to get the jump on other children and therefore on future competitors. The rationale is that the earlier the child begins taking up a sport, the better an adult athlete he will become. This may be true on the physical level, but rarely so on the emotional and psychological.

Child athletes who "burn out" early are an example of this. The above attitude takes little cognizance of the child's needs, as well as its emotional and physical well-being. Proponents of the "early start" theory of athletic development usually demand, or at best encourage, that children begin to develop motor skills. Obstacle courses might be set up to help the child to enhance balance, agility, and strength. This early practice is harmless and possibly beneficial for the child's sensory and muscular development. Developmental psychologists believe that children must be in an encouraging and stimulating environment in order to thrive in all of their sensory modalities and capacities. The subtle and at times severe attitudes behind parents' encouragement and pressure are the concern here. The hidden message may be that the child must develop athletically or its worth will be diminished in the eyes of its parents.

Many children unconsciously realize that their parents carry both joy and resentment in regard to their own athletic experiences. They may have failed in their dream to be a skater, a dancer, a fighter, or a football player. They may have been ridiculed in the school yard, or not been chosen on playground or organizational teams. They may have made such teams but rarely saw action. Such parents are often psychologically scarred as a result of these painful experiences occurring at highly vulnerable times in their own development.

Athletics is a proving ground for coordination, grace, power, dominance, social acceptance, peer respect, and sexual appeal. To be left out of this arena, with all its potential rewards, has to affect a youngster's feelings of personal adequacy. Anger and jealousy are common emotions among those who see others getting all of the acclaim and recognition. Any youth who considers himself a failure or who has been passed over in terms of athletic rewards is going to psychologically bear some ill effects.

Parents are going to form certain opinions and conclusions about sports and the value of trying to be a success at anything as a result of personal experiences. Parents may conclude that the intrinsic values of sports are health, coordination, competition, sportsmanship, and discipline, for instance. They may either reject or affirm secondary rewards such as fame, wealth, ego enhancement, or sexual popularity. On the other hand, they may decide that athletics is a frivolous and meaningless waste of time. Some former athletes, as well as nonathletes, end up with very cynical feelings towards sports because of their frustrations over discovering that their accomplishments did not provide them with the ego fulfillment they had anticipated. Conclusions drawn by the parents will be brought into their home, and the child must confront these and attempt to steer a course through them.

The parents' attitudes toward their past, family, careers and lives constitute the atmosphere of the home, and affect the child's sense of self and feelings about people and the world. The meaning that sports has for the child emerges out of the interactional network of values and beliefs that make up his or her world. Every child, without exception, must confront parental expectations. This occurs in every dimension of his or her life — religious, sexual, academic and athletic. The sportive dimension can never be totally disengaged from the others mentioned above.

As children, we are shaped by the interaction between our natural endowments and the environment into which we are born. Many athletes end up in a sport not because they are best suited for it or because they want to, but as a result of parental wishes, the family's economic condition, and societal or peer pressure. Many little boys would take up dance or tennis if given the opportunity, but feel pressured to participate in contact sports like football or basketball to prove their masculinity. (A father's insistence that his son take up a sport can often be traced back to serious flaws in his own personality and feelings of self-worth.) Little girls are encouraged to take up sports that emphasize grace and beauty; these embody qualities traditionally considered female. The child often does *not* end up in a suitable sport because he or she is too young to know better. A child's need for parental approval is critical; many times children pay the price of foregoing their own inclinations in favor of trying to fulfill their parents' expectations.

Some children may be discouraged or forbidden from participating in a sport because of their gender, the cost (skiing, tennis, dance); the inherent violence of the sport (boxing, karate, football, ice hockey, rugby); or the danger (surfing, car racing, motocross, parachuting, skateboarding, hang gliding, hockey). Others are encouraged into these very sports in order to prove to their parents and others that they are tough, or that they are just a chip off the old block.

What drives parents to orchestrate their child's athletics? They often need to compensate for things they do not get in their own lives, especially at work, such as respect, approval and recognition, and the accompanying feelings of worthiness. The child is often the second hope for the parents. Everything that a parent did or didn't accomplish in life is often asked of the child. If the parents achieved athletic success, then the child may not be expected to become a star athlete. If not, the same child may be asked to achieve greater success or status than the parent.

Parents, either due to circumstances beyond their control or more typically because of their fears, laziness, and cowardice, often abandoned their athletic dreams prematurely. Their failures usually gnaw at them for the entirety of their lives. The regret and remorse of an athlete who has unrealized dreams are often tremendous. One way to salvage their self-respect is to produce a child who succeeds where they failed. In this way, they are redeemed from their failures.

It would be interesting to know what Ray "Boom Boom" Mancini's motivation was to take up boxing and to push it all the way to the world championship. His father narrowly missed obtaining such a boxing crown years before. Getting as close to the top as he did, Ray Sr. was probably haunted by the championship that he never obtained. Through years of reflection he may have realized that some aspect of his training, choice of managers, and mental attitude may have significantly interfered with his quest to reach the heights of his profession. Either out of love for his gifted son or for personal gain and equilibrium, he may have felt that he knew how to take Ray Jr. to the top. He may have felt that he could show his son the traps along the way that usually torpedo most unsuspecting fighters.

Children, by nature, are extensions of their parents' identities, and their accomplishments may justify a parent's entire life. Having good and successful kids often makes parents feel that they are good and successful people. If a son becomes the lightweight boxing champ of the world, this obviously reflects on his parent(s). If a parent produced, trained and guided him to the top, this says something about the quality of the parent. The child and the parent in this case are not separate individuals, but a unit, a reflection of one another. With a fighter like Ray Jr., the love and concern he had for his father was so great that he would have died for him, and at times he seemed to fight with just such an intention.

These feelings are natural, but not always in the best interest of the child. Parents frequently relate to their children as reincarnations of themselves or as their followers, not as separate individuals. Many parents feel personal satisfaction, which they could not achieve in their own lives, through the child's successes and accomplishments. They lacked the talent, opportunity, discipline, dedication, and guidance that could have pushed them on towards the realization of their dreams and the actualization of their potential. There are several possible explanations why they did not achieve their goals: lack of family support; a substandard economic situation; the need to work to survive; and personality conflicts with coaches or others in authority. They may have ended up, through improper guidance and poor judgment, in a sporting environment that demanded they change their style of play, in essence their personality. There are many reasons why people fail, but it is rarely from lack of talent. Ninety-nine percent of the populace never put themselves in a position to find out just how good they are. They end up in the wrong place at the wrong time, playing it safe, copping out, or not facing the fact that even with 100 percent effort and dedication there is no guarantee that they will succeed.

Because there is no guarantee of success, most people either cripple or supercharge their athletic performance and hence their athletic career. Feelings of inadequacy can be devastating to an athlete who lacks a strong psychological foundation. Many parents, however, demand of their kids what they couldn't do. The wheels of destruction are set in gear: The child and parent, within such a dynamic field of issues, are destined to collide. The child, in this situation will realize that all the love and attention he or she is getting is to revive the parent's damaged ego. Discovering this will hurt the child, and on some level "break its back" emotionally. The child will figure out that trying to excel in order to fill in the gaps of the parent's identity is wrong. Instead of building a strong sense of self and a loving relationship with one's parents, the child's athletic career and relationship with his parents will deteriorate. If the child does succeed athletically, it will be a pleasureless undertaking.

Many parents become upset if the child does not have the same enthusiasm for sports as they do. Some interpret this as the child rejecting the parents. This reaction will have serious consequences for the parent/child relationship, but more importantly for the child's unfolding personality. He is trying to grow with the serious handicap of one or both of the parents having a negative attitude towards his feelings about athletics. Some parents subconsciously feel that children are a threat to them, because they are not reinforcing the parents' values and aspirations concerning an important area of their lives.

Many parents have children for less than ideal reasons; whether single or married, they feel lost in the harshness and complexity of the world. In conjunction with this, the limited nature of one's personal resources and circumstances (family, culture, and so forth), causes people to feel overwhelmed. They feel little sense of specialness or uniqueness. They don't even know why they are or should be living, let alone why they should try to maximize their personal development and athletic potential. They just can't handle life, let alone their dreams. People are drawn towards relationships (one of which is having children) and career paths in order to fill in these gaps of feelings of emptiness that result from not knowing how to live in an ultimate sense. The resulting impact on our soul and personality can make or break us.

Often we feel unimportant, just another average personality struggling to survive. Our fears of committing to something and not attaining it influence us not to strive for what we are best equipped to do, or fulfill our dreams for success. Just by nature of being a human being, we can only accomplish a fraction of what we dream of. This is often depressing and debilitating, and drives us mercilessly toward security and complacency.

Individuals also marry and have children because this gives them a meaning outside of themselves. Often, however, these people don't take up the slack of their own individual existences. They don't struggle enough prior to their marriage to achieve their fullest potential. This struggle *is* tiring and people often give up at a certain point. Parents often lay this burden onto their children; with their birth, the parents' old dreams reemerge with added vitality and are projected onto the kids. This is extremely dangerous because of the nature of the parent/child relationship: Children are so eager to do anything to win their parents' approval, they will become the standard-bearers of their parents' dreams or will try to atone for their past mistakes, regardless of how impossible the task.

It is very dangerous for those parents who feel like failures, or who feel shortchanged in life, to have a captive audience at home. Few people can keep in perspective that their children look up to them like a king and queen because the children's very lives depend upon currying their approval. They look to their parents for love and nutriment, and to be their mentors in life. Children want and desperately need to be loved by their parents. They long to discover and perceive their worth, specialness, and loveableness reflected in the eyes and actions of their parents. Neurotic parents often reverse this dynamic and expect such a response from their children.

In this situation, both sides are looking to be appreciated by the other. Unfortunately, the child is in a disadvantageous position: he or she must also strive to fulfill the parent's unmaterialized dreams. To repeat, the child will do just about anything in order to receive the life-giving sustenance of his parent's love. Such a setting is where the child's personality, with its resulting flaws due to the disproportionate demands and pressures put on it, forms. It is within this horizon that the child's budding sports identity is formed.

Parents unconsciously look for their child to carry the burden of their former athletic careers. The dad who was a physically weak or inept athlete may have tremendous resentment towards "jocks" in general. He may have over-compensated for his athletic inabilities by hyper-developing his intellectual skills. Despite his success in other fields, he may have a great deal of remorse and embarrassment concerning his athletic past. He may find secret pleasure in the fact that his son has athletic potential, and feel fulfilled as a man because he could produce such a son. Hence, his manhood, if not guaranteed, is at lease salavaged. He may either subtly or blatantly push his son to athletic supremacy in relation to the severity of his pain around this issue.

The same father could also act differently toward his son by holding him down, shaming him or just making it impossible for the kid to focus on sports. He may feel worse about himself as a man because even his little boy surpassed him athletically. His feelings towards his daughter's athletic inclinations and accomplishments will depend on his overall relationships with women and the daughter's choice of sport.

Because this father is probably ambivalent, he will simultaneously appreciate and resent his son's athletic gifts. He will give his boy a barrage of mixed messages concerning the meaning of sports, which will result in confusion and anxiety for the child. Such confusions will most likely remain unconscious; they will haunt the boy and take him off balance emotionally for the entirety of his athletic career.

The familial constellation around sports is even further complicated by the presence of the mother with her own personal history, views on sports, and needs in regard to her children. The mother may feel that sports are a waste of time, a frivolous undertaking. She may feel overwhelmed by her household duties and neglected by her husband. She may, for instance, resent her son's constant training and lack of help around the house. The son may receive from the mother much of the pain and anger that is meant for her husband. Similarly, the mother may have definite ideas of what her daughter should be doing with her spare time. This may or may not include athletics.

Both parents may be jealous of the son's and daughter's notoriety and popularity stemming from their athletic accomplishments. Recognition from sources outside of the home can be perceived as quite threatening to the parents' attempt to hold the reins on their children, keeping them emotionally dependent. Positive reinforcement from others facilitates independence and thus separation from the parents. The loss of parental control for certain needy parents can be quite frightening, and have serious side effects for the child. The possible ways that a parent can react to a child's athletic interests and successes are numerous, and add up to a very hazardous path that the would-be child athlete must traverse.

Athletic success typically opens many doors for the athlete at any age. Competitive athletes (especially in the college and pro ranks) travel, meet many different kinds of people, receive notoriety, achieve status, popularity, and money. Children become less dependent upon their parents for their feelings of importance and self-worth; they receive scholarship offers and chances to train with coaches in different locales. These accruements typically aid an individual's feelings of self-importance and emancipation from the family.

Some parents may resent the child's ability to break the strings of dependency. They may either consciously or subconsciously make the child's life very difficult, especially in regard to his or her athletic career. It is here, on a day-to-day basis, that young athletes are destroyed. The child may receive constant pressure that too much or not enough time is being devoted to sports. Some parents (not supportive ones trying to raise a well-balanced child) come up with many reasons why an aspiring athlete should curb his or her inclinations. They may feel jealous and inadequate in relation to their child's athletic accomplishments. Parents may be jealous that the sport can give the child so much pleasure and fulfillment *apart* from them. They feel impotent because they cannot affect their child in ways a bouncing basketball can. This is quite significant and is very revealing about the status of the parent-child relationship. These parents wonder how a game of shooting a ball through a basket can compete with the potentially rich and life-affirming energy that can pass between a parent and a child if the relationship is mature and mutually respectful.

The damage done to and pressure forced onto the child by the parents are usually subconsciously motivated. Parents are typically unaware of their own insecurities, inadequacies, and most importantly, unfulfilled dreams, be they athletic or not. Much of their communication about it comes out in subtle and therefore damaging ways. The parents weave a web of expectations and demands around the kid, typically using the withholding of love and attention as their ammunition. The child, without the analytical and reflective equipment to make sense of these demands, is bounced around like a ping-pong ball. All children know is that rewards, love, and attention come with certain actions and are withheld in regard to others. They do not know the deeper significance of their parents' reactions to their accomplishments on the playing field. They only know that their well-being depends on reading these cues astutely. There is, therefore, a dance being choreographed by the parents for their children. The only problem is that the steps are not clear from the start. Children learn them only through trial and error, and most often after failure.

The same dynamics described throughout this chapter exist even more primordially outside the area of athletic aspirations. Sports may be the test track or the battlefield upon which these are lived out. The child's sense of self-worth and belief in his or her ability to achieve gets structured very early. If a child is beaten, abused, or ignored—physically and psychologically—throughout the early years, he or she will be carrying a heavy burden which will most likely destroy any chance of success, no matter how courageous or how much the child is dedicated to training.

This can apply to a young girl who has been told brutally that she is worthless or bad, which equates with the message that she can't succeed or achieve, or doesn't deserve success. Such actions tell her that she is unworthy of happiness, and destroys any sense of adequacy or self-esteem. With such a strong message being broadcast daily, how can she possibly succeed? How can she slay this demon that has intertwined itself throughout her deepest feelings of self? Athletically, how can she realize that her style of training, choice of nonthreatening coaches, defiance of authority or folding under pressure stems from the hate and life-destroying image she received from significant others when she was defenseless and unable to sift through these distorted messages? Her response to pressure will be a stylistic reaction that may have helped her survive at home but is often inadequate for interacting with the rest of the world.

Let us now track more precisely the different developmental levels that a young athlete's career passes through and how familial and societal feedback comes to structure the mentality, style of performing, and level of competence of a struggling athlete.

Preschool Years

The preschool years are an important time in which fundamental patterns of interaction with others are set up. The child learns, in a worst-case scenario, that love and affection are conditional upon 1) meeting the expectations of parents and important others, and 2) performance. Children get the message that it is not acceptable to be who they are. They must achieve and perform well in order to be treated with respect, and therefore feel valuable in their own eyes. In relation to the severity of the demands placed upon them, children may develop fiercely competitive attitudes that border on the fanatical. Other athletes, friends and competitors may come to be seen as the enemy who threaten to take away their place in the sun and thus their refuge of personal worth.

Perhaps athletics is one place where children feel competent and appreciated. Fellow athletes may be seen as those who can steal their source of love and well-being by defeating and therefore reducing them to failure status, something they are vehemently struggling to avoid. The child's home environment may have conveyed the message that failure is shameful and intolerable. These kinds of feelings will create an atmosphere of such gravity and tension that athletic progress becomes nearly impossible.

There are so many pressures on a child. The pressure to excel may cause many children to forget about their personal reasons for being involved in sports in the first place. Their mission becomes the salvation of their parents', and their own, self-esteem through athletic accomplishments.

Parents are the initial and most powerful influence in the child's life. Their state of mental, physical and emotional health, and personal fulfillments, will be absorbed by the child. The child will learn very quickly just how important sports are to the parents, and will use this knowledge to ensure survival and place within the family. A child's athletic inclinations and preferences will be in direct proportion to the parent's athletic identity and needs. The child's own aptitudes and the availability of certain sports environments will also play a decided role in the choosing of a particular sport.

A child may also rebel against either the overt or covert pressure that the parents are creating. Many children choose certain sports that are in direct opposition to the sports their parents would prefer they go into. Such a move sets up a unique set of dynamics that is going to affect the child's accomplishments and performance in sport and probably rattle the parents' directives or increase their abhorrence of certain sports. These children will move into sports without much support from their parents. Parents often fail to recognize that kids demand to be treated with respect. If they are related to as second-class citizens, they will retaliate against those who are perceived as domineering and selfish, and who fail to acknowledge their needs and unique personality.

Here is an example of this kind of problem: A child's mother and father may desire the child to be a football player. They may exert tremendous pressure on the kid to take up the sport. Their reasons may include wanting the son to be manly, make lots of money (football can offer substantial financial rewards and the possibility of college scholarships), follow in the father's footsteps (the goal here may be to capture the dad's lost dream or to defend his reputation as a man and father), and achieve notoriety: Football in American culture is probably the most status-oriented of all male sports.

The child may react to the parents' desires in this situation by choosing ballet or tennis. The choice will be a direct statement to the parents. The boy may feel that the only way to assert his individuality, sense of power, or self-esteem is to use whatever circumstances are available in order to fight his oppressive parents. He chose, in this case, to disappoint his parents through the choice of sport. Children will always make the parents pay a price for oppressing them, in this case by dashing the father's dreams of football glory for his son.

Children may go into sports because of natural inclination or in opposition to the parents' placing great pressure on them in other areas of life (intellectual, academic, musical, and so forth).

Children, when rebelling, will always pick those behaviors, whether vocational or athletic, that most powerfully and directly affect the parents. When they feel oppressed and dominated, they will react and ultimately resist. The typical response is acting in a way that brings about disappointment and short-circuits the parents' dreams and aspirations for them. Rebellion is not freedom for the child, but a reaction against someone else's clearly defined and powerfully enforced position. Choosing a sport for rebellious reasons is far from ideal; it is the product of the family's interpersonal dynamics. The child's athletic performance will ultimately be in direct proportion to the intensity of these dynamics. The greater the psychological pressure during the formative years, the greater the child's chances of failure will be.

There are many issues of importance here: The boy mentioned above may desire to play football, but may feel that such a choice would put him in a subservient position with his overly enthusiastic parents. Choosing ballet or tennis from a position of defiance or rebellion is definitely going to affect the child's motivation and performance in these sports. He is set up for failure or burn out because the motivation comes from a stance of opposition. Attempting to progress in ballet or tennis is a counterproductive movement. The child has not chosen the sport freely and with the correct motivation. The sport has become an indirect, albeit neurotic, form of communicating the child's needs, feelings, sense of individuality and personality to the parents. He lives out this communique through his actions, and has very little conscious and reflective awareness of what he is doing.

Within such a framework, the child's love of the sport is either nonexistent or secondary to the leverage that it exerts in the communication process with the parents. In essence, the issue of sport as play becomes nonexistent. The child is unaware of this. All he or she knows is that there is a sense of tension and urgency that surrounds the chosen sport every time it is performed. As the child gets older, he or she will begin to realize how little fun all this is. Sports becomes a personal issue set within a family context; in essence, a battleground.

Unfortunately, most of the dynamics are typically unnoticed on both sides of the parent-child dyad. Both sides are usually unaware of the messages that are being communicated back and forth around the issue of sports. This state of affairs plants seeds in the child's unfolding self-concept and sports identity. These will take root and sprout throughout different stressful periods in the athlete's life. These early parent-child interactions are constructing a sense of athletic self-worth, with all its strong and weak points.

This is a very unfortunate situation. If these dynamics were more up-front and visible, they could be acknowledged by both parties. There would be far less anxiety, confusion, bitterness, and most of all, damage. Each side would react with every resource in its power, know what it was up against, and then make provisions accordingly. Such a situation, though, rarely exists in reality. Most families don't run on honesty, directness or mutual respect for each other's rights. Families are run, especially at the early stages, by the needs, desires and emotions of the parents. The rights of children are almost nonexistent, and usually have to be fought for. Often, if the child tries to be direct with the parents about how they are pressuring him or her to live up to their expectations, this only makes life more difficult.

If the parents are straight with the child and take responsibility for their actions, this will set a powerful precedent. The child will expect them to be consistent and continue this kind of dialogue or relationship. Those parents who need their children to justify their existence will not play fairly or give their child such an important role in family affairs for fear the child will take control of his or her life. Since the open type of parent-child relationship is atypical, the child will only communicate indirectly, primarily through action. This unconscious communication will typically stay underground until puberty because of the child's lack of experience, knowledge and "firepower." He will accept the status quo of the family structure as the only game in town, one which can only be played by certain long-standing rules.

Adolescence

In adolescence, the child can begin to crack under the pressure of increasingly more difficult training and competition, and failure to progress can be traced back to these earlier family dynamics and pressures. Children learn how to handle conflict and discover their own strengths and self-worth through interactions with others, primarily their parents. If their version of reality is never reinforced and validated when it is expressed, then they will never develop self-confidence. This is a vital constituent of top-flight athletes, and they will fold like a house of cards without it in the face of competitive pressure. The collapse will be due to their inability to develop a strong sense of identity and the dependable coping skills necessary to get them through the rough times and allow for adaptive and successful responses.

Sacrificing individual needs in order to please others lays the groundwork for a shaky, dependent and covertly resentful personality. Not allowing children to make decisions about their athletic careers, and thus to grow and learn from their choices, guarantees failure. Failure will occur mainly because their mental constitution is structured in a weak, distortive and flawed manner. It is only a matter of time before they crack under the intense pressure of increased competition. The resulting stresses, if they are not to be debilitating, must be handled by personalities that can prioritize (marshal) the time and energy from other areas of life in order to meet the ever-increasing demands of top-flight competition. Shaky identities cannot find the "stick-to-it"-type motivation to cope with such demands. The reason is that they are psychologically off-balance or damaged. They are pulled between wanting to realize their own unique personal characteristics and living up to their parents' version of who they should be. These athletes are trying (unbeknownst to themselves and others) just to keep emotionally afloat as opposed to tackling the difficult issue of athletic supremacy.

Much of young people's attunement to the world is unconscious. They make choices the conscious mind is not aware of. Frequently the choice of a sport, and how they will train and perform, have much to do with how they feel about themselves and how this relates to the expectations and importance of others. Self-worth, early in life, is directly related to a child's relationship with his parents. How a young athlete handles the pressures of his sport has much to do with his original intentions for choosing the sport; the support received from his parents; and what subconscious needs are fulfilled by participating in this sport. The deep psychological effect these personal dynamics have on an aspiring young athlete and would-be adult must be examined.

Any young athletes whose sense of self-worth is derived from athletic achievements are in serious trouble for several reasons. The children's personalities are going to be unbalanced: they may be insecure about personal appearance, academic abilities, or social skills. These may be left underdeveloped because the children devote little time to their growth. They are not allowed to develop their true talents and inclinations but have to live out a charade. As a result, they may flee more and more into athletic achievement in order to cover up personal inadequacies and emotional scars due to relationships with their parents. Unquestionably, a child who has very demanding, domineering, oppositional, or apathetic parents is going to be flawed deep within his or her personality. Such children will be confused and frightened to the core because they are unsure why their parents do not respect their rights and individuality. They will, more importantly, have doubts about their own intrinsic value and right to self-determination. Losing, or failing to develop, these qualities will send shock waves throughout every aspect of their lives and unfolding personalities.

Having to bolster an unbalanced identity may force the youngster to invest very little time in the less developed parts of his or her personality. Sports success is the "manna" that keeps the child emotionally fed. The child will, therefore, both resent and crave all the adulation received for athletic accomplishments. He or she will lap up this attention because it is the primary source of emotional nourishment, while resenting the donors. The child feels that it is too hard to work to get this attention and that it leads to an unhealthy "life course." He or she feels compelled to perform and achieve to be treated with the proper respect.

At some point, children will begin to question people's motives and intentions for liking them. They will feel that in some way life is a farce. People offer love and attention but only because the child performed and lived up to their expectations. The youngster may come to feel that these "love-givers" do not know the "real" child, only the part that performs. Children will wonder what love means if it is only based on accomplishment and an image of who they are. When increased pressure makes the game tedious, they will resent those they are emotionally dependent upon. The youths will hate them, but to fail or give up the sport would be to surrender their primary source of self-esteem. Such a foreclosure of emotional support at a vulnerable time in the child's life could be devastating.

A youth will willfully cling to the sport until its joylessness and drudgery become unbearable, and at that point he or she will burn out. This decline will evolve over time, and will include more than just athletics. It usually involves a breakdown of the major dimensions of a youth's self-concept, especially the ones constantly under pressure. These kids often have more at stake in their sport than just being a star performer; their emotional life is also involved. Failure under this tremendous pressure can cause repercussions for the remainder of their and others' lives.

Sports can bring attention to the child within the hierarchical structure of the family. It is well-known that children compete for their parents' attention. One very powerful way that children do this is by plugging into the parents' conscious and unconscious messages that they will reward a child who participates and excels in sports.

Every child has an insatiable appetite for parental love, attention and respect. If parents are offering a lot of goodies for athletic performance, most kids will jump for the bait. Children are very aware of parent-sibling relationships. Little Joey may notice that his brother, Bill, in failing to be a good football player, lost something special with his father by nature of being the oldest son in the family. Joey could treat this as an opportunity to gain esteem in his father's eyes, to take by force his older brother's position in respect to the father.

Depending on Joey's psychological needs, he may drive himself, neither for the pleasure nor glory, to curry his father's affection. Such a motivation is going to set a certain tone for Joey's athletic career. He may be terrified of failure, become obsessed with training and winning, or become alienated from his fellow athletes because they are perceived as potential competitors who could reduce him to second-class citizenship in the family.

There are many variations on this theme. Another possible way for Joey to react to his brother's athletic failure is that he could avoid sports altogether, so as to not end up in a similar position and lose whatever status he already has in the father's eyes.

Viewing his talents, he might consider it too risky to enter into competitive sports. Joey may even be the one with the talent and genuine interest in sports. He may only get involved, for example, in intramural sports, where there is much less at stake.

Joey may have also observed through Bill's career that his mother consistently reacted negatively to his brother's aggressiveness and "win at all costs" attitude. She may not have respected Bill for his brutal way of taking up the game, and may have withdrawn slightly from Bill emotionally. The father could have either taken a similar or opposite view of the same situation. Whatever the parental perceptions are, the young siblings become aware of these feelings. Let's say that Joey's issues are with his mother. He is very needy of her love and attention, possibly because she is a domineering and unaffectionate woman. He may then forego football so as not to displease her, or if he does take up the sport (in order to please his dad), he may try to be a "perfect gentleman" on the field. His fair-play style has its roots in trying to appease the combined expectations of his parents.

Another variation is that a child may fear to compete with an older sibling's athletic success. The child may avoid sports altogether in order to duck this issue, or choose one an older sibling is not, or has not, been involved in. The flip side of this is that a "hungry," hard-driving sibling may see the chance to achieve supremacy in the athletic hierarchy of the family by surpassing an older sibling's athletic reputation through head-to-head competition. The family dynamics and the child's feelings of affinity or alienation toward them will decide which alternative is chosen.

Sibling rivalry speaks to one central issue that a child will meet in a more extreme form outside of the home: There is only so much attention to go around in a family. Kids have to and will compete for it. They will grab onto every parental cue as to what they need to do to receive this attention. They will mark out their place in the family and have their needs respected by all the family. Once the child gets to school, the same process of marking out a "claim" increases. The young athlete has already learned at home that athletic success brings power and influence, whereas failure can sometimes result in ridicule and anonymity. Regardless of which message children receive at home, they will take their athletic skills and knowledge of how others have reacted to their success, or lack of it, into the competitive environment of grammar school. By this time, children know that sports are more than just a game you play for fun — they are a powerful avenue to recognition.

It is a fact that most young people today know they must compete and perform in order to establish their rightful place within the family, their school and the culture at large. The ability to compete, while taking into consideration a myriad of social issues (such as allegiance or cooperation), lies at the root of much of the child's sense of personal worth and ability to fit into a social matrix. This allows him to receive the rewards that special interest groups and society have to offer.

Many adults fail to tell a child that often people's love and admiration depend on performance. This is a very powerful message, especially when it is implicitly given to children by people they respect and need: parents, coaches, and teachers for instance. Children begin to realize subconsciously that much of their interpersonal support system is contingent upon their performance and fulfilling adults' expectations. These include how they are supposed to act, achieve in school, and perform on the athletic field. The damage is done, though, when the parents give this message unconsciously and then consciously tell the child that their love is unconditional.

Sport is so high-powered in the United States that children are inundated with sports coverage from every level of the media. They get the message that sports mean power from television and the reactions of their parents to the media. The meaning of power will change considerably as the child matures and realizes what life has to offer at different stages in his personal development. As we shall see in later chapters, the demands of performance and the pressures from significant others provide the impetus behind the child's movements towards success and the degree of ability to confront failure. People handle pressure when they have been prepared and groomed to handle it, rarely before.

Unfortunately, so many children in the United States today, average as well as gifted, live the tortured lives of entertainers. They must frequently prostitute themselves in order to fulfill the demands of certain important adults. Children cannot afford to lose or alienate their parents beyond a certain point. They are too needy and dependent, like budding sprouts with insatiable appetites

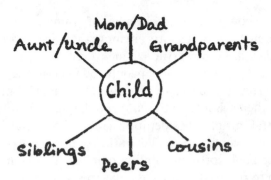

Family constellation.

for nourishment. Their life force is driven by the need to survive. People's basic quest today, because of modern medical expertise, is rarely physical, but emotional and psychological, survival. Children from the beginning are in a disadvantageous position. They must grab onto whatever will feed them and help them achieve maturation.

Children cannot be too choosy about what they take in. The foundation of their identity, with its ability to meet challenges and confront limits, is laid in the early years. Much of a child's self-esteem is based on accomplishment (especially sportive) and how this pleases certain people. This way of obtaining self-esteem is typical, but it is quite vulnerable and susceptible to being crushed by the uncertainties and failures that are a part of life. So many athletes are destroyed by failure or the inability to deal with perceived setbacks. It is the failure to live up to an ego ideal or distorted self-image that devastates athletes. When their false images fail to be affirmed, the athletes are thrown back on their emptiness and lack of personal substance. It is at these times that they do not know who they are because for years they had abandoned themselves by creating false selves to please others. These moments of identity loss are so frightening that they will most likely throw themselves back into their sport with renewed determination, in order to regain their sense of self-possession. Any gains an athlete makes under this kind of pressure will be shortlived. Pressure to please others to the exclusion of one's own needs and preferences leads to destruction.

Life is much more complicated than any book can describe,

and what has preceded is somewhat of a simplification. The issues described are true to life, but they rarely occur in isolation. The situation is usually much more complicated. A family is a system of relationships, and children will be influenced and receive input from everyone in their extended family. Also, they will commonly receive more than one message from the parents and anyone else who has input. The messages will probably come in many forms — some direct, others in a more subtle or unconscious form.

For example, the father may have come from a very athletic family. The child's grandfather may have been a professional or an all-around athlete. The father's brothers were talented boxers, wrestlers, and equestrians; one was an All-American and a two-sport professional. On top of this illustrious athletic legacy, the father was a talented wrestler, boxer, halfback, and catcher.

The father now has children and encourages his first-born son to be fit and competitive, and to learn discipline through sports. These are all qualities that any aerobic sport can offer. But, the father may not support the child's desires to take up dance because it is considered too effeminate. These are the father's overt messages to the child, but at the same time he cautions the child to beware of dedicating his life to sports, for this can be dangerous. Stories proliferate of the uncle's personal ruination due to a career in pro sports. His crushed knees and eventual death due to alcoholism have a powerful effect on the would-be athlete.

These stories are replete with many powerful and subtle messages that an impressionable and sensitive young child will pick up: The father speaks with pride and exuberance of his family's athletic accomplishments. The child will see, regardless of what the father says, that sport is a foundational dimension of the father's identity and feelings of virility. The child eventually hears of his uncle's demise and his father's decision to abandon a career in professional sports in favor of the more stable and less risky world of business. There are more serious and meaningful things to do in life besides athletics.

These contradictions will plant ambivalence and crack the foundation of the aspiring athlete's motivation for competing. He will always be in conflict and thus not able to give 100 percent attention and effort to his athletic task. A failure to be totally focused diminishes the chances of success.

A conflict has been set up in the son's subconscious. He sees that the father respects and admires athletic prowess and is proud of his own athletic success. As the son increases his dedication, however, the father starts undermining him. He tells horror stories of the collapse of former athletes, stops attending the son's athletic contests, and subtly pressures him to increase his studies and rewards him more for academic successes. The son begins to suspect that the father is secretly delighted in his athletic failures because it keeps alive the father's dream of his son's eventually going into business.

The son is being pulled in several directions. He is trying to gain his father's respect, but because of the contradictory messages, he is unsure which path to pursue wholeheartedly. His chances of athletic success within this kind of conflict are negligible. More subtly, though, these warnings about the uncertainty of an athletic career are going to burrow deep within the son's subconscious, largely because the warning has a basis in reality.

Everything in life involves a risk. The son is not told this, but only that athletics falls into this category. It is quite probable that the child, having been influenced in this way, will always hedge his bets in terms of his sports career so as not to get crushed by failure, but doing so only increases his chances of failure. This ambivalence may influence the athlete to avoid top-flight competition, or never structure and increase his practice time in order to work on all aspects of his game. This prevents him from developing his strengths and always puts him in a static state. The athlete may train, choose competitors, coaches, and teams that will protect rather than challenge him to be his best. Subconsciously, the athlete views such challenges as just providing the opportunity for defeat and failure.

To complicate matters and make them more true to life, this boy may be subtly ridiculed by his mother for his dedication to such an unimportant and meaningless endeavor as basketball. His brothers and sisters may be jealous of his athletic success and in particular his position and esteem in the father's eyes. The siblings may continually find many blatant and insidious ways to tear at the boy's sense of self and place in the family. He may end up feeling like a stranger in regard to his siblings. They most typically will play off the parent's ambivalent feelings in regard to his athletic endeavors and attempt to create a number of crosscurrents of tension that the son must deal with. The message is that even the people whom he is closest to can either reward or subtly discourage him. This is a tough problem for a child, let alone an adult to figure out. It will usually lead to confusion, despair and athletic collapse.

The above is one short example of how complicated the family structure is in regard to a budding athlete. There are a multitude of ways that these dynamics can constellate, in regard to the particulars of each family. The bottom line, regardless of the specifics, is that this complex of interpersonal dynamics will undoubtedly influence the tone and flavor of the child's identity and athletic career.

These early dynamics will set the pattern and greatly influence the child's chances of optimal athletic performance throughout life. Much of these early and implicit messages from the family, coaches and players will be the strings upon which the demands of ever increasing competition will play.

The sad part of all of this is that top-flight athletic competition is a brutal world. There are few winners and multitudes of losers. Many athletes, as a result of what has been described so far, are driven by forces outside of their conscious awareness. They are under continuous pressure to excel. Their very livelihoods and feelings of self-esteem depend on performance. This is a vicious environment: Drugs, nervous breakdowns, alcoholism, insanity, and suicide are often the price of trying to reach the upper echelons of the athletic world with identities that are unstable and inadequately prepared.

The attempt of this book is to show how the mind of the athlete gets structured in so many finely nuanced and complicated ways in these early years. These structures will break under increased stress somewhere along the youth's athletic ascent unless the foundation of his personality has been well laid. Many athletes end up sabotaging their own careers and performances because, like frightened and driven animals, they are unaware of why they are taking up their sport in the first place, what they receive from it, who they are trying to please or fulfill, and how their fragile sense of self is contingent upon the rewards and praise they receive from others in regard to their athletic accomplishments. *These* dynamics, in relation to the strengths of the athlete's identity, determine how well an athlete trains, performs and learns from temporary setbacks (injuries, personal crises, and failure to achieve goals in a specified time period, for instance). In this context, the athlete's mentality is crucial to athletic success. The next chapter deals with the nature of competition and how it affects the unfolding of an athlete's personality and self-understanding. Competition provides the setting for the installation and rigidification of the aforementioned neurotic personality dynamics.

2
Coming Up Through the Ranks

All young athletes must encounter many new sports environments as they climb the competitive ladder. Every age and
level of competition makes different demands. In order to progress
to the next and more demanding stage of competition, the athlete
must work through the challenges offered at each previous level.
This chapter briefly traces the issues and pressures that young
athletes must cope with at each stage of their athletic development,
and presents a clear picture of what they are up against emotionally
and psychologically as their athletic careers progress. Also examined is how their sense of identity and level of confidence are
shaped through the stresses they encounter as they climb the competitive ladder.

Preschool

As mentioned in the previous chapter, children initially make
their first contact with the world of sports at home, through the

family. Eventually, around the age of three or four, they begin to play in the streets or local playgrounds with siblings or friends. Some may even begin formal training with coaches at this time, in skating, dancing, gymnastics, or skiing, for instance. Such an early beginning is not at all rare.

Moving to the streets or the playground is an important step for every child. Leaving the security of the home, they now begin, in a fledgling manner, the process of socialization and testing their skills against other children. Children begin to meet and learn to deal with others from different family backgrounds (ethnic, cultural and physical). Through play, they begin to develop physically and mentally, and understand how people interact and get along. Children learn how people form rules and guidelines to insure proper interaction; this protects the rights of all those involved in play. These interpersonal dynamics of play that are learned at this age will have long-lasting effects throughout the athletes' personal evolution and ascent. The rules of their environment are duplicated in their playful interactions. The rules of "ghetto ball" are pretty much the same as those of ghetto life; strength, style, effect and intimidation are the rules of "playground basketball." The basketball court is a semisafe replica of the streets.

Similarly, through play, children begin to rehearse and develop muscular, emotional and psychological capacities. They are testing their bodies, minds and emotions, trying to see what they can do with their talents. The preschool years are essential for the beginning athlete. Children are becoming acquainted with their bodily skills and the guidelines that surround playful social interaction. They are also learning how to gain ascendency through competition.

This is also a time of forming friendships and relationships. Peer respect and cooperation are important at this age. Children learn that regardless of how talented athletically they are, cooperation and playing by the rules must be learned. Rules are typically mutually agreed upon by the group. Ideally, they speak of justice, fair play and respect for the rights of all those involved. In reality, however, rules are formed by the strongest and most capable members of the group. In spite of certain dominant children, playing by the rules insures that each child will be included in the group. This is very important to the average child, and quite difficult for an aggressive, talented one to learn. The latter child has the strength and skill to set the pace, and may resent having to play by rules that protect less talented playmates.

This concept is very important to children. They have just ventured outside the safety of their homes, and are anxious and afraid of this new, unknown territory. To feel liked and appreciated in this new environment has a calming effect on them. They will be encouraged to venture further into the world of strangers and group participation. The benefits of social success and harmony will probably encourage children to explore the world of competitive athletics.

The preschool years can be a trying time for children: They are given some autonomy by their family, a chance to do things their own way without parental observation. They are not supervised as much as when they were toddlers. This allows them to start developing their skills in their own unique style. A conflict arises because they worry about alienating important people in their lives (parents and friends) through their attempts at emancipation.

Understandably, play is very important at this age. It allows children to develop, in private, the way they want to do things. Simultaneously, they can observe how other children handle certain tasks and crises. Without the anxiety of having to please watchful adults, children will begin to freely experiment and give expression to their unique gifts and perceptions.

Children do not need many goals and much discipline at this stage. A safe, noncompetitive environment allows them to work on their skills in a low-pressure and nonjudgmental atmosphere. To force a worklike ethic on the child could be disastrous. At this age, sports are play, a game, a physical expression of the child's expanding sense of what he or she is capable of. Dreams of stardom, one hopes, are a long way off for the preschool child.

Grammar School

As the child enters elementary school, the world of sport changes again. First through third grades are still caught up in the world of the playground. With each passing year, though, certain children wait eagerly for the time when they can play on a team. This is a major turning point in the career of every athlete. Once on a team, the child learns that for most coaches, winning is the primary concern. The playful, unstructured climate of the playground becomes a thing of the past. The introduction of a coach brings with it an air of seriousness. Sports become somewhat less fun but more exciting, depending on the coach's mentality. The stakes are higher and so are the rewards.

Many new dimensions are added to the sports world at this time. Parents, teachers, coaches, cheerleaders, team spirit, and school pride become part of the impetus behind grammar school sports. Children clearly get the message that sports are important and that there is much hoopla and prestige surrounding them. They learn this from television and first-hand experience. Children begin to realize that they can become minor celebrities, not only among their peers but with neighboring parents, coaches, and teachers. By excelling, they can carve out a place of eminence for themselves and receive preferential treatment. Less gifted or less mature athletes, conversely, can be crushed by failures at this time and end up feeling quite inadequate and inferior. This is a time when children lord their athletic prowess over one another. It is the first time they have a chance to separate themselves from an adult-dominated world. These feelings of competence and power are very inebriating for young people, who up to this point in life have had to admire and envy the power and competency of the adults around them. The children now get a taste of power.

Children whose athletic abilities do not develop until much later are often scarred emotionally by their failures and limitations. Sometimes, these emotional injuries last a lifetime. Feelings of inferiority often surface later in life, profoundly affecting people in ways they never completely transcend. Timing is very important. If a child's strength, coordination, and speed come late in life, he or she may get lost in the shuffle. Success in grammar school may not have been possible for some children, and this could leave such a bad taste for sports that they might never risk competing again, in any activity, for fear of failing.

As children grow older, the caliber and organizational structure of athletics become more complex and intense. Little League, Pop Warner, recreation leagues, youth soccer teams, Bobby Sox softball, and AAU swim teams become alluring attractions for budding athletes and their parents. Medals, block sweaters, league championships, and all-star teams are the bait that hooks many young athletes, their parents and coaches. These are the tangible symbols of *public* success, and do not speak to the private emotional state and well-being of the athlete. For highly pressured athletes, the best that can be said of their successes is that they have learned dedication, discipline and sacrifice; no one can take these qualities or their medals away from them. Children who use the success of athletics to gain love and approval may perceive their medals and trophies as tangible evidence of an enhanced self-worth that is not felt internally or within the family structure. These public symbols cannot be taken away at any whim the way their parents' approval can. The athletic burner is quickly getting hotter; for all athletes, the emotionally healthy as well as unhealthy, the desire to improve increases with the acquisition of success and its rewards.

With each passing year of grammar school, children are traveling farther from home and meeting fellow athletes from different backgrounds. If successful, they are growing in self-esteem that is independent of their parents. These changing dynamics are beginning to take hold of and shape the children's unfolding self-understanding and sense of personal worth. The successes, disappointments and failures of these early competitive years are quite influential. Children are quite impressionable at this age and have few other forms of reference in which to learn who they are. Sport, for some children, becomes the preferred and exclusive medium through which they begin to define themselves. Feeling that they are a winner or loser can decide how they perceive their chances of athletic, academic, and eventually professional success. The core of one's identity, at this time, is either being embellished or diminished with the passing of each year.

High School

Toward the finish of elementary school, every serious young athlete is thinking of high school competition. This offers exciting but scary possibilities. Few children realize that along with the greater prestige and attention given to high school athletes, the competition and rules by which one's teammates and coaches play are more intense. Every child, regardless of grammar school reputation, has to prove him or herself anew. Upon entering high school, adolescents learn that their bodies are beginning to go through radical changes, growing and developing at different rates than others their age. Young adults begin to either pass or fall behind one another. Self-image, self-worth, and feelings of athletic competence are in tremendous upheaval and transition during this age. The unfolding of a youth's genetic blueprint can have serious consequences, depending on its timing in relation to the normative standards and demands of the culture.

In the United States, athletes are introduced to professional coaches at this time. They are professional in the sense that this is the way they make their living. Their professions, incomes and feelings of self-worth are invested in being successful, which typically translates into *winning*. A professional coach's influence on developing athletes cannot be stressed enough. Adolescence is a time of great uncertainty. Youths are trying to establish or maintain their athletic and personal reputations, define what it means to be male or female, and establish some kind of competence to prepare themselves for the ever-increasing responsibilities of adulthood. They are often rebellious and defiant because they are vulnerable, disoriented, and impressionable. Adolescents are urgently trying to form an identity and life of their own; they are still confused about who they are and what they can become.

Young adults are looking for role models to pattern their growth after. If they are aspiring athletes, their coaches have a tremendous amount of power and influence over their athletic careers *and* overall feelings of self-worth, confidence and identity, especially if they have most of their self-esteem wrapped up in athletic success. If this is the case, the coach is holding the strings of their lives. If the coach is perceived as a threat or an enemy, the adolescent will withdraw emotionally, quit the sport or rebel through defiance or passive/aggressive behavior.

This power given to coaches begins much earlier than high school. In many ways, coaches have the single most powerful effect on an aspiring athlete's career and emotional life. As stated earlier, many children are not playing for fun, but for emotional stability within the family. Since young people spend enormous amounts of time with their coaches, as their competitive levels increase, coaches can be more influential than parents. With so much power, they can encourage, even destroy, a youth's career and belief in self.

Adolescents looking for guidance from sources other than their parents may become more invested in their athletic careers than anything else, and they may look to their coaches to supply reinforcement and validation they may not be getting at home. Parents rarely realize that many coaches are emotionally unbalanced. They may use their position of authority and influence to bolster their unfulfilled identities. Many coaches are frustrated athletes who have never dealt with or gotten over the nonrealization of their own athletic dreams. They usually have many unresolved issues concerning their sport and their identities. Unfortunately, many youths receive the backlash of these coaches' frustrations, most often in a covert fashion. A coach is typically not aware of what he is expressing through his actions, and the sensitive athlete, without much psychological insight or experience, tends to personalize much of what a coach says and does. A coach's damaged ego can cause the athlete to suffer emotionally.

More young athletes have been ruined by coaches than any other single factor. Parents and athletes must be alert to this fact, and realize that what happens to a person in an athletic environment can affect his or her personal and family life also. A great deal of personal tragedy and wasted talent can be avoided if parents take the responsibility, especially with children dedicated to athletics, to make sure that their coaches are emotionally stable and sensitive to their children as individuals. Technical proficiency should be sought out later in the child's career and not be the number one priority at this time. Skill acquisition is crucial to athletic success but there are other requisites that should take precedence.

There are coaches who are downright wonderful. They are caring, giving, knowledgeable and sensitive to the physical and emotional needs of young people. Some of the most precious memories of any athlete's career are probably connected with the personal relationship that he or she had with a special coach.

High school is a time when adolescents are searching for their individual identity, but at the same time trying to be accepted and included by their social group. This is a *very* difficult tension to maintain. Peers become the youth's primary concern. Adult authority figures outside of athletics are often delegated to a role of secondary importance. Adults are beginning to be looked at critically and more objectively. Their perceptions and commands are not accepted blindly just because they are adults. Adolescent defiance is partly due to a youth's ability to stand up and fight against that which is perceived as oppressive. Acquiescence is not as common as in grammar school. Adolescent athletes want to develop their own style and be appreciated for it. They need structure and guidance, but also room to move, develop and execute their athletic selves. Their uniqueness is demanding expression and can no longer be held down without negative consequences to their self-view and ability to perform.

Personality clashes and power conflicts with coaches are going to increase at this time. The athlete–coach relationship is one of the single most important dynamics of athletic success. Adolescents trying to win the regard and esteem of the adult world will give their heart and soul to sports in the hope of currying their coaches' love and appreciation. Adolescent and adult sports often center around the athlete's feeling for a coach, and their performance will be consistenly better over a long period of time when playing for a coach they like and respect.

Sports at this stage are becoming more like real life. Adolescent athletes are practicing more intensely and longer than they ever did before. They are having to budget their time, learn discipline and organize their activities. They are beginning to realize that if they want to be good, they are going to have to specialize, even drop other activities and sports to concentrate and focus on one in particular. This is very difficult because adolescents are trying to decide who they are and what they want to be. They do not want to make an incorrect decision about a sport they are devoted to. Young athletes are terrified about making commitments at this point in life because they want to keep their options open. Life demands that athletes make decisions while they are trying to decide what their strongest interests are and in which area their best chance of success lies. They are concurrently getting advice and pressure from parents, teachers, coaches, and friends to meet *their* expectations. Whatever choices are made will by necessity exclude other desired possibilities. Anxieties over making bad decisions are commonplace during this age. Ambivalence can lead to emotional paralysis and destruction of one's athletic career.

Athletic success in high school also enhances popularity and attractiveness to members of the opposite sex. The bloom of puberty carries with it the explosion of hormonal and sexual changes. The allure of sex and the entree into this world are added incentives for the youth to participate in athletics. This is especially important for adolescents seeking out members of the opposite sex to get the attention, affection and overall response that are lacking at home. At the other extreme, participation in athletics is a perfect opportunity to avoid the whole world of sexual issues — dating, intimacy, sexual experimentation, caring, loss, and so on. By pouring all one's time and energy into sports, the timid adolescent is insulated from this interpersonal world. Athletics can be a refuge for the tentative, awkward, introverted and troubled youngster.

Finally, many high school athletes are thinking about college sports. It is not just ambitious coaches who know that college is a place to build a reputation. At this point in their careers, athletes are introduced to the dog-eat-dog world of competitive athletics. For many, this is a shock. They begin to realize that even their closest friends are only concerned with their own reputations. People are out there fighting for themselves, and this is a rude awakening for many naive and innocent athletes. This gives some adolescents such a bitter taste in their mouths that they quit athletics altogether. The joy and fun of childhood athletics have been *irretrievably* lost. This shock, in conjunction with the destructive and at times ruthless influences of certain coaches, ends many careers before their time. This often occurs when coaches ignore the emotional needs of the athlete and focus solely on the technical and physical part of the game. The athlete's identity is passed over in the name of tangible or superficial adjustments. Many times these refinements fail to make a difference in the athlete's actual performance because some deeper psychological need or conflict continues on unaddressed, neutralizing one's best efforts.

Many coaches at all levels fail to recognize that athletes are not just bodies that perform. They are people with developmental histories and anticipated futures who most importantly react to all coaching directives within their personal frame of reference. As shaped by the athletes' feelings of self-worth, problems with authority figures and motivations for achieving only tangible rewards (to the exclusion of technical proficiency) will influence them to react to coaching directives either seriously, apathetically, passively, or rebelliously.

Most adolescents, especially young athletes, are not emotionally prepared for the ruthlessness and competitiveness of the adult world. One of their first introductions into this world is through athletics. The transition from the world of play to that of production and results is rarely explained to children, however; they are usually not prepared for it. The function of rites of passage in many primitive cultures is to prepare youths for the transition into the adult world, preparing them to live by rules they are not used to. This does not happen in modern society; the transition scares many adolescents, to various degrees, back to the safety of their former world. They resist and at times are terrified to move into a world where play and fun for their own sake are perceived as useless, immature, and a waste of time. Adolescents' emotional development may slow down, depending on the intensity of such negative experiences, in order to postpone entry into the adult world. They are not just physically moving from grammar school buildings to a high school campus; adolescents are entering a whole new world, with new networks of interpersonal relationships, responsibilities, and value systems.

College

In college, much of what an athlete experienced in the jump to high school athletics is intensified. Sports, depending on the collegiate institution, are a big business. Athletes are commodities who are paid (by scholarships, jobs, kickbacks, academic privileges, and training for professional careers) to perform and produce. Collegiate athletics are a money-making venture, a big-time enterprise. Television and gate receipts are often a university's largest source of income. As a result, winning and the reputation of the school are primary. Athletes are the cogs in the wheel of this juggernaut; they are of secondary importance and can typically be replaced at this level. Also, coaches' reputations, careers and livelihoods are on the line. Their contracts are usually short term and their extension depends greatly on the coaches' win–loss records. Their situation is one of produce or move on.

The college athlete is one of a select few. College is usually the highest level of amateur athletics in the United States. The potential rewards for athletes at this stage in their careers are enormous. Additionally, getting to this level of competition has demanded much sacrifice and in many cases has determined their future career possibilities. It is very hard at this point in life to abandon all the time and energy that athletes have put into their careers. The stakes are high, and the odds of achieving success are low. Here the cut-throat dimension of sports gets intensified. Many athletes are psychologically ill-prepared for the pressures of collegiate athletics; consequently, they fail. Many have trouble accepting the transformation of the game they loved as kids to a job and a means to support themselves.

Unless athletes are emotionally mature and understand what their motives are for being in athletics, their careers will soon bottom out. Largely due to immaturity, most athletes' motivations for being involved in sports are not linked to the changing nature of athletics. As they age from children to adults, athletes move from a world of dependence and little initiative to one that demands self-sufficiency and responsibility. Many athletes realize, too late, that the meaning and nature of sport (for those around them) have radically changed. Their motivation does not match the changes that have occurred. Sport is no longer fun, and they are also out of sync with those running the show. These athletes usually pay a heavy price for not keeping up with the times: failure. A possible exception is when an athlete has extraordinary ability.

The meaning and demands of sport are constantly changing for young athletes. Unless they, or those in a position to guide them, are aware of the shifting demands and influences, the chances of failure and psychological damage are greatly increased. Knowledge of these dynamics allows for the possibility of growth and fruition.

As athletes rise through the ranks, they are forced to confront their physical and emotional limitations. All the psychological messages that were communicated from parents to their children concerning self-worth are stirred up. Their typically unconscious motives for taking up the sport run aground when their natural abilities peak. At this point, athletes must be emotionally mature to develop and to get the most out of their talents. Psychologically immature, damaged, or unaware athletes will have great difficulty at some point in their careers. The ensuing performance plateaus, especially when athletes feel incapable of getting through them, negatively affect their psyches. This is especially true of the unconscious mental blocks that originated at critical times in their emotional development. It is at these times that all the damaged parts of the athlete's identity get stored up and kick into action full force. They frequently have the effect of subconsciously sabotaging the athletes' relationship with coaches and other players, their training and performance, and ultimately their careers. An athlete's most formidable opponent is too often him or herself.

All that has been mentioned above is so unnecessary. If athletes could be counseled and prepared for the different changes they are going to encounter with each jump to a higher level, they could be spared a great deal of needless anxiety and failure.

3
Competition

American children, from a very early age, are subjected to a great deal of competitive pressure. They must compete with their siblings for their parents' attention and affections, and against other children for their place in the hierarchy of the neighborhood or school ground. This is especially true of young boys. Traditionally, psychologists have noted that young males are geared toward struggle and competition with their peers, each striving for ascendency. Their self-esteem and unfolding identity are nourished by their status on the local male continuum, especially in terms of physical prowess and coordination. Young girls seem to be more directed towards affiliation and cooperation. Their emphasis is on relationships and inclusion by the local peer group. There is now, however, a gradual cultural shift in these dynamics and resultant gender behaviors. The rising influence of the women's movement in drawing attention to female athletics, coupled with male awareness of the drawbacks of a super-competitive approach to sports and relationships in general, has brought about a certain leveling of male-female behavioral differences.

Competition is everywhere, from the classroom to the neighborhood. Being at the top of the pecking order brings with it a basket of rewards. Children need and crave recognition. They want to excel, realize their potential, and reap the fruits of such efforts. Being better helps children to distinguish themselves from others. Achieving our goals makes us feel a cut above the rest. Anonymity and averageness are derogatory terms in our culture. Being like others in this age of individuality and narcissism is to be nothing; having recognition is to be somebody and ensures a place in society. Having a place carries with it a whole constellation of relationships to others. Everyone craves, on some level, to be recognized by peers, neighbors, parents, mates, and bosses. With esteem come respect, appreciation, consideration and privilege.

Children learn very quickly that in competition there is only one winner. They see this everywhere: on television, in the movies, magazines and books, as well as every other aspect of their lives. Television, especially, highlights this, whether it shows a boxing match or a 100-meter dash. At the climax, no matter how close the other contestants were to the victor, the camera pans on the winner, putting the vanquished off screen and forgotten. Second, third and fourth place finishers rarely receive accolades and commercial success.

Since losers are quickly forgotten, the message is that they are a dime a dozen. Society only recognizes winners and winning is the raison d'etre of most athletes. There can only be one winner. When push comes to shove only the winner, whose strength, guile and technique were superior on a given day will be left standing. This is life pushed to the limits, the glamour and attraction of competitive athletics. Performance counts, not talk. This is the wonderful and ruthless side of athletics. It is the one time, more so in some sports than others, that athletes get outside the pettiness of others' egos and the limits of having to deal with the bureaucracy of life. This is especially true when there is a clear and concrete goal, e.g., running the fastest 100 meters. Here the world's nonsense temporarily subsides and these runners are allowed to decide their own fate. They push their talents and trining to the max, without interference from anybody. The rewards are tangible, and not conditional upon politics, personalities, arbitrariness, or subservience to the mores of mainstream life. Competition on the athletic field frees people, for the most part, from these restraints, and is one of the main reasons people compete. Most people compete to satisfy their egos and psychological needs (which we all have), and to realize financial gain and fame. But, the chance to utilize their full abilities is what thrills athletes and hooks them initially. The world of sports is one of the few places left in the United States to allow this without interference. As every athlete knows, however, the higher one goes up the competitive ladder, the less the aforementioned holds.

If athletes competed primarily to test the limits of their abilities and to get into that "pure space," there would be many winners, not just for the moment (regardless of objective performance) but in life as well. No one would be forgotten because no one would have the need to be remembered. This is *not* the orientation of the athletic world, however; knowing that oblivion follows athletic failure (not meeting objective standards) is an extremely heavy pressure for young athletes to absorb.

The impact on athletes is tremendous. For instance, the 200-meter silver medalist in the Olympics may have been beaten by only a fraction of a second. On that day, five other runners might have been right behind him, but except for the first three finishers, they received no medals, nothing except the tremendous honor of having run in the Olympics. These eight runners were some of the best in this event in the whole world — maybe in history — but only three individuals were officially recognized. A contender rarely walks away from a race not feeling like a failure, or more importantly, sensing the absurdity of his life's choice. The athlete has probably spent the major part of his life training for this event; the dedication and sacrifice are mind-boggling to a nonathlete. He reaches the pinnacle of his sport, something that few of us ever do in any dimension of life, yet because he did not win, he is ignored, passed over in regard to monetary recompense, job opportunities and athletic immortality. The gold medalist (in certain prestigious events) has the world at his feet, at least for a short time, not unlike a bull-elk establishing dominance in his herd. The loser is left to wander aimlessly through the tundra alone and vanquished until he is able to summon the courage to continue the struggle once again.

Children learn that everyone loves a winner. They learn very early (especially when they confront their limits and superior competition) that life at the top is very tenuous and dangerous. Not

only is everyone gunning for you, but all the fringe benefits—
respect, privileges, attractiveness to members of the opposite sex,
and so forth—are contingent upon performance. Whether this
situation is bad is not the issue. The reality is that this is the way
the American culture is set up. The damage is done when adults
(parents) soft-peddle this fact or do not tell their children explicitly
what they are up against and expected to cope with. The harshness
of this reality doesn't hit a talented athlete until the early or late
teens. When the caliber of competition rises sharply and players'
ego needs begin to dominate their style of play, then the impetus
moves away from a team approach and towards an individual style
of play. This is also a time when teenagers are being faced with
many life issues, such as the choice of colleges, careers, financial
responsibilities, and sexual partners. Sport is quickly becoming a
business, and young people know that the stakes are getting higher
all the time.

Many teenagers are quite naive, unaware of the gradual intru-
sion of the adult world, with its many concerns into the world of
sports. Competition becomes more and more intense without the
youth realizing what the driving force behind the whole athletic
scene is. It is like waves hitting on the beach: One coming in, the
other going out. Children are jarred by the clashing of these two
worlds, their youth and forthcoming adulthood. Depending on
what is driving them, children may push ahead deeper into the
struggle without really having any idea why they do so or what they
are up against.

Children are also naive to the callousness and brutality of the
world. Superior athletes ride the crest of their success with few setbacks until they meet top-flight competition. Even though they
have seen teammates pass by the wayside, few are touched by the
fact that their number may come up also. When they fall, they fall
hard, without adequate coping skills to soften their crash. A fall
into anonymity after being up so high can be devastating. Some
never get back up or on with the rest of their lives.

Somehow sensing that the sports world is brutal, many
children who are bypassed early develop a fear of sports. They
receive a heavy dose of reality too soon. Feelings of incompetence,
at critical times in children's athletic careers, can be devastating to
their sense of values and self-acceptance. Rather than risk such

humiliation again they may put the whole business on the shelf. Others may continue to battle the competitive currents as they rise to the top because they are terrified of failure and ending up in the same predicament as their fallen comrades. Such pressure may influence them to perform cautiously or avoid pressure situations and dangerous competitors (in other words, to play it safe). Still other athletes realize the pitfalls and dangers of failure, so they drive themselves mercilessly to avoid such situations. Their need is to dominate their opponents. For some this will bring tremendous rewards; for others, when they meet their match, they will be totally unprepared for a setback, and will fall like a rotten oak in a gale wind.

Today many young athletes' feelings of well-being come from athletic success. If these children are raised by pressuring parents, the game borders on Russian roulette. Unless they have the talent, tenacity and discipline to go all the way (which few do), they are going to become quite neurotic and unbalanced, at worst emotionally crippled or destroyed. To fail with so much pressure may be experienced as a disgrace from which they cannot recover. Most often youths will hyperdevelop their athletic skills, usually only those that are needed at this point in their careers to excel. Their academic, social, and dating skills may be neglected. These children become lopsided, trying to cover over the inadequate or less developed side of their personalities with athletic achievements. They become "junkies," their whole lives structured around the drug of sports success. Just like a beautiful woman who doesn't have to work on the underdeveloped parts of her personality (despite several failed relationships) because there is always another eager suitor waiting in the wings, successful athletes cruise through many interpersonal conflicts and crises relatively easily and with less trauma than their nonsuccessful counterparts. Unfortunately, this "unfinished business" will catch up with the athletes eventually.

As these youths mature, they will have failed to develop in several major areas of their personalities. They are vulnerable to falling apart when failure, injury or tragedy hits their lives. The coping skills are not available to handle such setbacks and the significant impact they have on self-esteem. On some levels, the further athletes go, the more they become aware of this unbalanced state of affairs and their susceptiblity to being emotionally crushed by the pressure and conflicts of life. This only adds to the already increasing amount of pressure athletes are under from others and themselves. These pressures affect performance even more than technique and top-level conditioning.

Parents and coaches do not realize that many children enter the sports world for reasons other than just to learn coordination and have fun. Many are like kamikazes; mediocrity is a disgrace, a shame that they may never be able to erase. Sport might not be enjoyable because of the overemphasis on competition and winning. Coupled with parental expectation and pressure, children are trapped.

Competition is tricky. Children who become overly competitive for unhealthy reasons might risk alienating friends and family. They possibly resort to cheating or dirty-play in order to win. More typically, athletes will overtrain to the point of being counterproductive. They become emotionally and physically depleted, and are often vulnerable to physical injury and emotional traumas. This is understandable, for to some children, losing is failing; to fail is to be nobody, unworthy of love, warmth, and attention, and may also lead to obscurity at home and school.

Many children who have put such a high premium on athletics to salvage their identity often feel somewhat worthless or unworthy of love outside of their athletic achievements. They feel that if they don't succeed on the playing field that no one will have any reason to be around them. They learned at an early age that they were only loved and given attention when they won or were above average; to lose meant being ignored and possibly cut off from those they loved. To lose is to fall from a state that we all desire — grace. In this state, everything is a gift. We have to do little to receive the love and adulation of those around us. We just need to be ourselves. Unfortunately, few people receive this kind of attention and usually have to perform well, in the face of continual expectations, to get their loved ones' attention. Success involves a tremendously high price, as the athlete often is driven by emotions and conflicts she or he has little awareness of. Such conflicts, and how they are dealt with, distinguish the top-flight from the mediocre athlete.

It is impossible to abstract the athlete out of life, something that contemporary psychology and traditional sports psychology attempt. Athletes are not research objects that can be studied in isolation; they are highly invested in the world of their own involvements. Their feelings of self-esteem are often conditional upon the love and support of those important others whom they share their lives with. Only looking at physiological response levels and relaxation techniques misses the boat. Those aspects are important but not at the foundation of athletic performance. The meaning that sport and all its accoutrements have for athletes and those they are significantly connected with lie at the core of their identities and structures.

The higher athletes go on the competitive ladder, the more influential the psychological factors are on their capacity to perform, especially under pressure. The greater the stress and pressure, the greater the odds that the weak links in the athletes' self-worth will be exposed and collapse. Athletes form themselves in day-to-day living. Answers to the following questions explain the role emotions play in performance: Why do some individuals have the ability or single-mindedness to practice diligently, to execute proper technique, day in and day out? Why are some athletes' performances so erratic, sometimes reaching greatness and other days characterized by lethargy? Is it just that all athletes have their good days and bad days? The stresses and strains of day-to-day living affect one's chemical constitution, but the biochemical explanation for inconsistency misses the point. Many great athletes were always "at it," for example Muhammad Ali, Sugar Ray Leonard, Boom-Boom Mancini, Edwin Moses, Julius Erving, John Havlicek, Jerry West, and others who always rose to the occasion even if they were not at maximum efficiency. The answers to above questions lie in the state of their minds, their well-being, that enabled them to always "be on." Understanding the mentality of the superior athlete will be the focus of the remainder of this book.

The majority of athletes, gifted and not-so-gifted, are buffeted by their unconscious needs, expectations, psychic scars and life presures. Most of these dynamics are played out, or find conscious expression, in mood swings, drops in energy levels, feelings of boredom, lack of discipline, inconsistency in training schedules, susceptibility to injury, inability to play with pain or discomfort, and most important, "choking." These behavioral characteristics are the result of intrapsychic conflict. These athletes are not integrated with themselves, and have not made peace with their lives and reasons for being in the sport. This state of affairs is the strongest influence in an athlete's sports life, with clear ramifications. Athletes who are pulled in so many directions are the rule rather than the exception.

Young athletes are driven by their parents' and others' expectations; how they subconsciously deal with these pressures buffets, drives, and tortures them in ways that they don't understand. All they know is that they are not succeeding and that in some vaguely understood manner they are sabotaging themselves. They are unaware of their true motivations.

Children are like water, adapting to the contours of their environment, for better or worse. Their goal is to survive in any environment, competitive or not. They will play by the rules of the home, neighborhood, or school, because initially, those are the only rules they know of. The more they play by them the more their mentality (conscious and unconscious) will be structured according to these rules. Eventually, the strengths and weaknesses of these structurizations will show up. These weaknesses and the messages that have gone into their subconscious about their self-worth will constantly, without letup, pick away at their attempts at excellence until they slump in a confused huddle by the side of the playing field. Many such athletes will be damaged permanently. Sadder, though, is the waste of their talents. If somewhere along the line they could have been advised as to what they were facing and what was driving them, they might have achieved athletic excellence. Athletic expertise is valuable largely because it makes athletes proud and gives them a positive feeling about personal identity and capability. They learn the value of taking risks and pushing to the zenith of their abilities. In some ways, the meaning of life and personal fulfillment is living without regret, in the knowledge that one did the very best possible. This is the most profound aspect of competitive endeavors, but is not the primary focus in the United States.

Children are immersed in a competitive world where *results* are the primary concern. Personal growth and development are largely an offshoot of sports. Coaches and players put these aspects in a subordinate position to winning. The further children go in athletics, the more they will have to realize that the athletic world they are struggling in is concerned with only two matters: victory and success. Their personal lives and development are something they will have to care for on their own. The ignorance behind this attitude, often held by coaches and administrators, is ridiculous. The athletes' chances of athletic development and victory decrease when emotional and psychological development is ignored.

Competition *forces* athletes to confront their limits, weaknesses, and strengths. It is one place in life where it is hard to hide personal liabilities. For this reason, it is extremely important that an athlete be brought along slowly and with proper guidance, much like a well-handled novice boxer. Such a fighter is never forced to face an opponent who has superior skills. This way, the individual can mature gradually and avoid running into a "sidewinder" until he is ready to handle it. The chances of success increase tenfold when an athlete is allowed to grow physically and mentally at his or her own rate.

Next, we shall look at what sustains an athlete through the stresses and strains of the competitive world, one that bluntly states: You're nothing unless you are a winner. The motivation of athletes can either nourish or cripple them as they journey through this brutal world.

4
Motivation

We must now try to understand what the forces are that propel athletes. So far we have looked at environmental (family, peer, social, and school) pressures that growing athletes encounter. How the young athletes react and process these pressures in order to create motivation will be the concern of this chapter.

Athletes are unique in their reasons for taking up a sport. The issue is that athletes, especially budding young men or women, are deeply affected by the wishes, needs, and demands of the people that are most essential to their personal development and feelings of self-worth. The pressures from home, incorporated with the demands to succeed, be popular, rich, powerful, or attractive, exert a profound influence on their motivation and approach to their goals in sports.

People's minds, especially those seeking excellence and success (athletic or not), are quite complex. There are many levels upon which one's sports motivation is grounded. Human beings rarely do something, especially requiring great expenditures of time and energy, for just a *single* reason. Athletes rarely make all the sacrifices they do for just one of the following: money, popularity, accomplishment, victory, or love of the sport. Typically, all of these motivators are present to varying degrees of importance. Some of these will be more figural or important than others, for different athletes and at different times in their careers.

Athletes, typically, are not consciously aware of why they push themselves. Also, the fundamental and most powerful of athletes' motivators come from their families. These influences constellate around feelings of worth in their parents' eyes. This also holds true with feelings of lovableness and desirability in respect to peers and lovers. Many athletes, unknown to themselves, are carrying within them the hidden messages of their childhoods. For example, depending on the structure of the family's system of relationships, the athlete might be trying to prove that he is a good child, adolescent, or adult, and therefore is worthy of respect, care, love and affection. He tries to prove his self-worth in the competitive arena. The athlete is terrified that he will be judged inadequate, worthless, or unimportant—a failure. This is the message certain significant individuals in his earlier years had conveyed to him both explicitly and implicitly.

These messages arouse apprehensions that are so deeply ingrained and subtly layered that most people are unaware of how much influence they have on their lives. Athletes are typically only aware of a subtle dissatisfaction and disquietude with their sport, lives, and selves. Their training becomes tedious, lifeless and boring. Every athlete, even the psychologically healthy, runs into periods that are seemingly nonproductive and pleasureless. Sometimes just the routinization of training and practice can try the patience and fortitude of any athlete. There are, however, many athletes whose motivation problems are much more serious. They have literally trapped themselves in their sport. The more of their lives and self-esteem they put into it, the harder it is to let go. The question becomes, Who am I without my sport? Mary Decker's reaction of anguish and rage when she and Zola Budd collided in the 1984 Olympics, possibly causing Decker's defeat, answers this question. The fear is that the athlete will cease to be important without her sport success and thus become a "nobody."

History books are filled with former great athletes who went from fame, success, and wealth to obscurity, failure and poverty. The ride to the top may take a lifetime, but the fall to the bottom can be rapid and final. Many athletes do not comprehend the fickleness and values of their adoring and paying public. They don't save, plan, and invest — emotionally or economically — for a time when they will be relatively average citizens struggling to get by. Much of this is because they are hooked on fame and what it does for their damaged identities. Many times these athletes are blind to everything but quenching this insatiable need, something that has its jumbled roots in a childhood where the love vital to growth was available in only meager portions. Until athletes become aware of this dynamic, they are doomed to a tortured and twisted fate on and off the athletic field.

There are many reasons in addition to naivete and lack of education for athletes' failure to plan. They are driven by psychological needs that are deeper than what is obvious to themselves and others. All athletes are driven by issues of identity. No one in real life dedicates himself to a game just for the fun of it. Motivators such as fun are not strong enough to push and sustain athletes through the painful gauntlet that must be run to reach the top. Such a path is fraught with tension, anxiety, continual pressure to stay in shape and on top. For these individuals, almost all areas of life must be structured around training. If people are in it for fun, they are either extraordinarily gifted, independently wealthy, or just plain crazy.

Athletic supremacy is a gateway to life's riches on and off the court. Success usually brings a great deal of material from which one can create and repair a damaged ego or enhance an already stable and strong identity.

Many athletes are driven by the need to feel good about themselves and to secure the blessings life has to offer. We all aspire for the latter. How badly we have to have certain things says much about where we've been and what we need to have to feel secure and at peace with ourselves in an increasingly complex, competitive and cold world.

We have talked already about why children and adolescents pick one sport over another. The reasons are varied, the choice offers a great deal to their evolving identity: their parents' affections, a specifically desired reputation; the possibility of securing for their family a better socioeconomic position, fame, and safeguards against obscurity, anonymity, and ridicule. Sport is a place where people can prove their self-worth and value to their families, friends and potential partners. Also, it can provide camaraderie, and an esprit de corps, which athletes of all ages and both genders crave.

The fellowship present in team sports such as basketball, soccer, rugby, football, gymnastics, and swimming can rarely be found anywhere else to such a strong degree. The existence of military commando units and other special units of the armed forces are exceptions to this.

In basketball, having teammates striving together for a common goal is exhilarating. The closeness, mutual respect and dependency the players experience with one another can surpass, at times, the feelings, closeness and bonds they have with their own families. Athletes fight for a common goal. Each athlete is a vital component. Family members are unfortunately rarely imbued with such respect and responsibility. Victory is not the only goal; the enhancement of the athletes' egos and the fulfillment of their abilities are also important. Many American families today are not united and do not struggle for a common goal. Family members are often out doing their own thing, and sports provide a young man or woman with a surrogate family and thus the emotional commitments so badly needed and so strongly desired at this critical phase of development. Athletes, in short, can receive more attention, respect, help, and care from teammates and coaches than from their own families.

Many children also latch onto a sport for what it will do for them independently of others. For example, karate will enable an individual to be more secure in the face of threats or manipulations coming from physical intimidation. Martial arts are also somewhat esoteric and have mystical flavorings. Training is serious, demanding and painful. Upon reaching certain levels of excellence, one attains an air of toughness, uniqueness, mystery, and respect. Any or all of these could be badly needed to shore up an individual's damaged or faltering ego; they are tremendously ego-enhancing and give that person an aura of power. Power in relation to others has been a driving force in all human affairs since time immemorial. An athlete, depending on the psychological structure of his or her mentality, may cling to a chosen sport with an intensity and tenacity that look unnecessary, even irrational, to the outside observer, in order to obtain these qualities.

Dance, similarly, allows the development of finesse, coordination, grace and aesthetic mystique. Such qualities may be desperately needed by individuals who feel that they embody the exact opposite. Additionally, some people need to be on stage, the center of attention. Their narcissistic cravings, due to overblown egos (pumped up or ignored by their families), demand appeasement. These feelings may be necessary to cover over terrible feelings of inadequacy, badness, or lack of parental love and acceptance. The latter could derive from messages that a youth consistently received at home — that the child was fundamentally bad, unlovable, or that he or she *had* to be a success to be treated with respect. This creates a tremendous need within the individual to overcompensate, to reclaim a feeling of self-importance that every child needs and rightly deserves. Hence, children embark on a dangerous and urgent quest to obtain recognition at any cost. At times, this quest is diametrically opposed to their own best interests. To them, adulation and recognition are as close to love and acceptance as they will ever know.

Recognition and adulation become, however, pitiful substitutes for the lack of acceptance, in regard to their personal characteristics, that they received from their parents at critical times in their lives, and for which they never stop hungering. Everyone tries to survive without these vital interchanges and affirmations. These youths will eventually discover that success, fame, money, companionship and even a certain form of love can be obtained through athletic supremacy. If they have the talent and the mentality to match they will, like any drowning person, jump on the sports wagon and struggle for all they can get. This depends, of course, on the severity of their hunger and how much they have been emotionally deprived and damaged.

Similarly, many youngsters choose running as their sport for a multitude of reasons. They do not have to be too tall or muscular, for instance. More importantly, running is a loner's sport: it can be performed on its own, for the most part. Runners, especially distance runners, are comparatively unrestricted, unlike other areas in their lives. They can cut themselves off from the masses, have privacy, a space to focus, and concentrate apart from the clatter of day-to-day life. There is also a meditative quality and benefit that come from doing a certain simple movement over and over. Athletes who are involved in covering great distances, such as swimmers, runners, rowers, or bicyclists, have to perform a repetitious movement continuously. They become addicted to their sport because of this kind of trance, or peak experience, and the lack of human pettiness that their sport provides.

All sports provide a multitude of benefits and reasons why people take them up and participate in them. There is a cluster of rewards that can be derived from sports: personal, interpersonal, emotional, and physical.

Another way to approach the issue is to ask, Why do some athletes thrive on competition and seek the toughest competition, while others avoid top-flight competitors or competition altogether? The answers, while keeping specific individuals in mind, will reveal why people choose a sport in the first place.

There are many individuals, even great athletes, who diligently train every day and never compete. Sometimes, this is because they love their sport and despise the nonsense of the competitive world. More often, though, it is because of past failures, having to wait too long for success, pressures from mates and family to give up training, or the need to do "something serious with their lives." As legitimate as these excuses are, the bottom line is that all athletes, on some level, are terrified of failure, being judged, and being found to be inadequate. The fear is that they will disappoint themselves and others, and feel that they wasted their lives. Inwardly, they will feel ashamed of failure or of not living up to their and others' expectations. The fear of being judged and found wanting is common to all people, and for some athletes, this fear is incapacitating during training, and especially, actual performance. These intimidating fears, and those of letting others down, can alter a person's whole approach to athletics. Obviously, the state of one's identity has so much to do with whether one will be able to risk failure and disappointment (whether temporary or permanent). The better people feel about themselves, the easier it is to pursue their goals and simultaneously risk disappointment in a particular area of life.

Many athletes fear that anything less than dominance or perfection is unacceptable. They must always win and perform at the maximum of their abilities. Being on stage and performing less than perfectly is seen as limited, flawed, or worst of all, just plain average. For some, this is devastating; losing means ceasing to exist for a time, feeling lost. Obviously, athletes who react this way to competitive situations are emotionally shaky and will rarely make it to the top. So many athletes, however, subject themselves to a tortured approach to sports because of influences and messages from others that have worked their way into their subconscious.

Knowing that athletes' identities depend on their athletic accomplishments says much about their approach and motivation. If the majority of their feelings of self-worth depend on athletic success, then they will have a very tenuous hold on their psychic equilibrium. Athletes can be buffeted by athletic accomplishments or the lack of them, and by the whims of coaches, fellow players, officials, and administrators. A dangerous game is being played because much of their self-concept is in the hands of others.

If these athletes have good relationships at home and with friends, a solid love life, and other pursuits (academic or artistic), they will have other areas of their lives to draw on in order to feel good about themselves. This is important: It provides athletes with a foundation of support in the face of athletic failures which all are, of course, bound to encounter again and again in their careers.

People who put their eggs in one basket are usually dependent on who owns the basket and who is making use of it. Many blossoming athletes are psychologically destroyed by their inability to deal with the demanding personalities of their parents, teammates, and coaches. Locking horns with these individuals, at a vulnerable time, can result in an athlete quitting and suffering serious psychological damage. Athletes who have a strong supportive and loving system of relationships in their lives usually feel secure and strong enough to handle these life crises.

Athletes primarily dependent upon athletic success for feelings of self-worth may be much more dedicated to a sport than those who have well-rounded identities. They need their sport much more and therefore are more driven and desperate to succeed. But they are also more psychologically vulnerable and usually very anxious when training and competing. Sport, for them, is not just a game, but a do-or-die experience. Their emotional lives and well-being depend on success, and they have great difficulty handling failure. These athletes are often crushed by failure because they are nothing without their athletic careers. They rarely have the resources to cope with a major crisis, whether in their athletic or personal lives.

Athletes such as these are in dire straits. At some point, their physical and mental skills will be matched or surpassed by others, putting their athletic capabilities to the test. This is an opportunity for the emotionally strong athlete to dig deeply, face his or her limits, find new potential, or push farther. Many athletes bottom out at this time, lacking the emotional stamina to adapt and rise to the demands of this new level of competition. This is the rule rather than the exception. Most athletes' identities are so fragile, unbalanced and therefore weak that they cannot adapt and be flexible enough to give up old ways of doing things, or modify their training practices. "Burning out" usually takes years but it is the end product of the aforementioned process.

For example, many athletes, particularly in sports that require less muscle power (such as tennis and golf), will resist getting into a serious weight-training program to build up their strength, something that is painful, time consuming, and requires much discipline and concentration. They might invoke the self-deceptive rationale, as many do, that being stronger is not the primary reason for their lack of success. Being in karate for over eight years, I know without a doubt that even in doing just technical forms, or katas, where the movements are soft and flowing, technique is improved 30–50 percent just from being physically stronger. Being stronger gives more control over movement and allows even the most gentle and light movements to be done with more precision and finesse.

Athletes resist change, in large part due to the structure of their identity, which is usually too rigid and defensive. They cannot give up the security of what they know how to do well to enter unknown territory and develop new skills. Most adults are painfully aware of what it was like being uncoordinated and unskilled as a child. Trying to learn something new — how to swing a bat or dribble a basketball — was frustrating and at times embarrassing.

Childhood, in addition to its carefree, positive aspects, is remembered as a time of incompetence, and of both admiring and resenting adult expertise. Children are often ridiculed and embarrassed by domineering adults for their fledgling attempts at sports and other activities. They spend much of their formative years trying to shake the stigma of awkwardness and incompetence. Once they achieve a semblance of control and finesse, they will do everything possible to maintain it. Being put in the position of a beginner again is too threatening to the identity of many adolescent and adult athletes.

In light of this, it is easy to understand why adults have trouble taking up and learning new sports. Many athletes' identities are so invested in being a star that they have tremendous difficulty in allowing themselves to be a beginner. This same dynamic holds true in their training formats. They do over and over the things that they are best at, but fail to initiate and practice new dimensions of their sport that would integrate the less-developed aspects of their style and abilities.

Some athletes are more concerned with looking good than with winning or success. They cannot risk looking less than perfect in a particular maneuver, and are too ashamed to be seen in any way or facet of their game that would be below their most competent form. This is very common in all sports, but I will use karate as an example to illustrate this point.

A fighter I know has a very good roundhouse kick. In sparring he uses it frequently and is quite successful with it against opponents at or below his level, but can rarely get the kick in against a superior opponent. The main reason is that he only throws the kick from his back leg, giving his opponent more time to see the kick coming than if it were thrown from his front leg. I have suggested a number of times that he learn to throw the kick off his front leg, feeling sure that it would be more effective. A year has gone by and he continues to throw the kick solely from his back leg. He will not learn to throw the front-leg version because he is one of my teachers and his identity is very much invested in this role. To accept my advice, in his eyes, would be to lessen his authority over me. His ego cannot stand to practice a kick, either in private or especially in front of his students, that is less than perfect. In short, he cannot allow himself to be awkward and average in front of his students. He gets better at what he already knows, but limits himself tremendously because of his inability to adapt and expand.

In order to develop new dimensions of identity and sport (which are vitally interdependent) people must allow themselves to acknowledge that at some point, they are all beginners and if they are going to grow it has to be from this point. If athletes try to cover this up, or pretend that they are better at a certain stage than they actually are, then they will not give themselves the opportunity to progress; be too anxious about performance and how others are viewing them, which handicaps their chances of improvement; and continually try to cover up their inadequacies. The repercussions of this kind of stance are counterproductive to learning and athletic growth. Athletes fail to progress in their sport and end up hiding behind the defenses and rigidities of their fragile identities. As their careers begin to fade, they can do nothing but watch in dumbfounded helplessness as the sports world passes them by. Being fearful can entrap and undermine not only individual natural gifts, but possibly a whole life of dedication and sacrifice. This is a waste of human potential.

The motivation and commitment of athletes to sport are grounded in their personal experiences and ideology of who they should and should not be in regard to their families and selves. It is foolhardy for athletes to train day in and day out without paying heed to the state of their mental health and personality formation.

Most coaches and players are reluctant to discover what lies in the recesses of others' minds. Everybody struggles to deal with his own life. If athletes are clear as to who they are, why they compete and why they resist certain facets of their game, they will be better able to maximize their potential and performance.

How this kind of inflexible mind-set short circuits many careers will be discussed in Chapter 6 (on Training). Such rigidity speaks to questions of identity, who I am for instance, or who I should or shouldn't be, and who I can be. Many athletes feel humiliated if they realize or are told they are not quick, fast, or good enough. Serious and dedicated programs of weight training and agility drills can improve athletic skills at least 20 percent. Truly serious athletes will invest the time and energy in an already hectic and draining day to implement such a program. Excellence is important to them, and they will pay the price to maximize their potential, while at the same time being able to leave the security of what they can do well for that which is new and allows for growth.

Once again, it all boils down to motivation: Without knowing their deepest motivation (the more subtle dynamics that fuel their athletic endeavors) athletes work against themselves. Those who know what and why they do it will have a decided, perhaps overwhelming, advantage over opponents. These athletes will look at themselves objectively and work on whatever parts of their game that need improvement and development. They will be maximally efficient, and not work against themselves and subvert their conscious intentions. Mentally aware and stable athletes with the necessary physical skills for excellence will be the prototypes of the future. This is the new frontier of sports. How the minds of the athletes influence performance will soon be the focus of all athletic training because physical and technological limts are rapidly being encountered. Every athlete knows that sport is largely a mental, not physical, discipline, especially when looking at the disparity of performance levels at the highest rungs on the competitive ladder.

In essence, motivation is the key to superior athletic performance, propelling and sustaining any consistent and disciplined effort. If an athlete is pulled emotionally by a multitude of stresses and demands (many of which he has repressed) to live up to some idealized self-image or to please others through athletic achievements, then he will be at a tremendous disadvantage. This will cause a rift in the core of his personality. He will be ambivalent, rarely feel at ease with himself, and his concentration and capacity to persevere in the face of adversity will be diminished. He will be easily distracted, internally and externally, by any signal or warning that his sense of self is about to be threatened or overwhelmed.

When these early-warning defense systems kick into effect, this athlete will do everything necessary to preserve who he thinks he should be in order to avoid anything that would disgrace him in his own or others' eyes. Unfortunately, this is counterproductive to a maximum athletic effort, and he will try too hard, thus getting out of his natural rhythm, or get so worked up emotionally by event time that he will be drained and apathetic. He has put himself in a situation where the likelihood of failure is greatly increased, the exact situation that his protective systems are designed to avoid.

A defensive posture will not only defeat him in the moment, but will burn him out over the long run. He will not be able to muster the energy necessary to sustain the type of concerted effort needed to take him to the pinnacle of his ability. Even the best of sentries can only handle limited guard duty when near enemy lines. As long as the athlete remains in this attitude, his capacity to perform freely and in response to the demands of any athletic contest, especially an important one, will be greatly restricted.

Knowing in the depth of his soul that he has the talent to do better, after turning in a subpar performance, only exacerbates the problem. If an athlete needs to maintain his self-esteem through superior athletic performance, he will be creating undue anxiety and pressure that most superior athletes do not have to deal with when trying to rise to the top. Too much pressure leads to "choking" and subpar performance, and continuing to perform below one's ability leads to shame and guilt. Initially, for many athletes, this may lead to a redoubling of efforts. When the pattern continues for very long it inevitably leads to a further reduction in the athlete's ability to perform. This cycle repeats itself until the athlete quits in disgust or from emotional and physical "burn out."

Emotional clarity and stability are essential prerequisites for athletic success. Talent, intelligence and proper conditioning are crucial, but without a strong emotional basis to stand on, the athlete's best efforts will be wasted. In other words, he will be driving that superbly developed body with the brakes on.

Athletes need to be aware of what drives them; this way, they can be more in control of their own destinies. If their sense of self is damaged and if they are subconsciously trying to prove something to others, they are on a course to disaster.

Putting an emotionally unbalanced athlete (most "normal" people fall into this category for the reasons stated above) into a prolonged, or even short-term, pressurized situation and forcing him to interact with other athletes and coaches, all with their own typically repressed psychological issues, make for a very heady brew. This offers countless possible ways for all of the parties involved to become emotionally off balance, thus having their chances of athletic success jeopardized.

Every athlete and coach needs to get emotionally clear. This means that each needs to get in touch with the many reasons he is performing and what drives or motivates him to take up the sport in the unique way that he does. Until this is accomplished, each is playing Russian roulette. If this emotional house-cleaning could occur, the savings in talent, time and money could be astronomical.

There are many personal conflicts and motives that athletes typically suppress or push out of conscious awareness. In actuality, there are really no totally inappropriate motives for achieving goals as long as people are able to consciously acknowledge what these motives are. Obviously, some motives are much more expedient than others, but in the final analysis the motive is objectively unimportant. What is crucial is that it is important to the athlete.

An individual might take up body-building because he feels vulnerable in the face of intimidating men; he is motivated for entirely appropriate reasons. On the other hand, if he represses this motive because he is ashamed to acknowledge his fears and insecurities, he is in trouble. If he tells himself, which is often the case, that he is only trying to tone up his body, then he will bail out when he encounters difficult training barriers and plateaus. The pain and sacrifice required to get over these barriers will not be generated by the desire to have a well-toned body. It must come from something stronger, something that will enable him to deal with the pain he is going to experience. If he can get in touch with the humiliation that he has had to frequently endure in the past and admit that he is fed up with being frightened and intimidated, then he will find deep within himself the determination to succeed and to do whatever is necessary to build his physical strength to the point where he can defend himself against all comers.

True motivation, that which has been forged in pain, disappointment, and in the fires of one's dreams, is hard to defeat. Unfortunately, most of us are too frightened to get in touch with our deepest motives because they are tied in with, and born out of, the depth of our souls. It is here that we have suffered, questioned, and been in despair concerning the tortuous path that we have and must continue to traverse in our lives if we expect to grow and get the best out of life and ourselves.

Getting in tune with these motives will put us in tune with the painful experiences that generated them. Most of us do not want to feel these things, so we create self-deceptive motives that are easier to live with. These do not provide us with the drive necessary to realize our dreams. If we could face the truths of our lives, then nothing could stop us. If, however, we deceive ourselves and hedge our bets, then mediocrity and the shame of constantly failing to live up to our potential will be our destiny. The choice should be clear.

People must be sensitized to the types of psychological issues and dynamics that prevent them from realizing their goals. Unfortunately, what has been stated above, which is at the heart of superior performance, is not being addressed by the athletic establishment in the United States. The Eastern-bloc countries continue to progress in this regard. It is time for us to wake up and stop letting this fertile domain of athletic performance go untapped.

5

Commitment

Commitment to sport largely springs from motivation and interest. It is very difficult to commit to something wholeheartedly; commitment constantly demands recommitment. The further athletes go into sport, and the more they give to it in terms of time, money, lost opportunities, and strains on personal relationships and academic performance, the more their original motivations and commitments will be tested and need reevaluation. Each jump in competition (high school to college, college to semipro and eventually professional) requires a reevaluation of motives and a reformulation of priorities. As athletes go up the competitive road, they must give up something in other areas of life. Most top-flight athletes painfully realize that others are out partying, dating, travelling, and eating rich food while they are training and keeping workingman's hours. There is little time for these pleasures; they can undermine training, health, and composure.

It is important, then, that athletes realize why they are in their sport in the first place. If their strongest motivators are unconscious, then they can be easily upset by the obstacles that will be encountered. The results of these encounters will be experienced as personality conflicts with coaches, interactions with competitors who seem to have them pegged and defeat them regularly, injuries, changes in coaches and teams, and problems in their personal lives. These obstacles can and do knock some athletes off kilter, and send some into severe depression. For example, an athlete may have a basic conflict with his coach's personality and orientation towards the sport. He may be unable to adapt and compromise, and may become so upset, full of anger, resentment, and anxiety that his game begins to deteriorate so badly that he is never heard from again. How does this happen? How can an athlete with so much talent, training, and promise bite the dust so quickly? It is not just because of stiff competition or oppositional coaches, but lack of motivation and commitment.

Players, especially young ones, do not realize they are not in tune with the intricacies of their minds and personalities. They are unaware, for instance, that the reason they cannot adapt to their coach's "mad dog" style of basketball is because their identity is so fragile that they perceive the coach as wanting to take it away. On a deeper level, the athlete's unconscious may see the coach as being like his or her parent — an authority figure saying you are not O.K. the way you are. Rightly or wrongly the athlete may experience the coach as saying, You must change the style of play that you have worked on for years and been successful with, just to please me. Certain athletes will refuse to give up their style on a coach's command — they may refuse to be what the coach wants them to be. Some athletes, depending on either the strength or weakness of their egos, can adapt to the desired format. Others, like the athlete in question, may decide to rebel. The main thrust behind such a rebellion is typically unconscious. Athletes usually have little conscious awareness that their rebellion has deep roots in their personal lives, especially in regard to domineering and demanding parents.

Such rebels are usually cut from the team or ride the bench. Despite not playing, they may feel, in a peculiar way, that at least they have not been dominated. But unfortunately by not playing, they usually ruin their careers. This is a high price to pay for such a shallow victory. Also, they might get labelled as rebels or trouble makers. Such labels do not help athletes promote themselves, particularly if they want to contract with a different team.

The opposite also occurs quite frequently. An athlete does not rebel but changes her style of play to suit the coach. Her willingness to change may be rooted in her history of being passive to authority figures, to curry the coach's favor, and to defuse the possibility of rejection and alienation. This athlete could also damage her career by such an acquiescence. She may adapt, but by squelching her natural style of play, end up being of little value in the present system, and could ride the bench as well. The variations on this theme are numerous.

Parents, friends and even coaches may try to talk to the player and put some "common sense" into her head, but they don't understand the depth and relative hiddenness of her motivation. Also, people closest to her may be personally involved in her problems and have a stake in keeping her in a subservient position in other areas of her life. Consequently, they have no desire to dredge up problems or pains that they might be partially responsible for, by supporting a change in the status quo or personality style of the player. Such changes would not enhance their desire to dominate the athlete.

Most people shy away from people in distress for the following reasons: They don't want to hear, feel or get caught up in their pain if they feel that they have been struggling to survive themselves, and have no desire to take on another's problems. They do not want to be affected by the athlete's problems because it may put them in touch with something that they have been trying to forget or avoid. They may have to open themselves up in regard to the athlete and acknowledge their own struggles, concerns, and confusions. Intimacy is a problem for many people; as mentioned earlier, the individual may have to take responsibility and own up to anything he or she has done that contributed to the athlete's present or past crises. Many people are implicated in athletes' problems. In most cases, depending on athletes' value to the team, they are usually left to sink or swim with their problems.

Athletes are going to have a great deal of trouble making sense of the whole dilemma in this atmosphere of apprehensiveness and lack of communication. The best they can probably do is ride the process out to the end in the only way they know. Also, their commitment to sport is, at best, going to be willful, that is, they will have to grit their teeth and try harder. Such determination may only sink athletes deeper. Recommitment, in order to facilitate future growth, must involve change and an awareness of the crucial demands of the situation. Compromise and reorientation will be involved. The only way budding athletes can bring this about is through insight into their motivators and what fuels their sense of self. Different issues (popularity, fun, excitement, camaraderie, and self-realization) can be at stake depending upon their activities, because athletes want to please both their parents and themselves. These motives are obviously quite different. If athletes feel supported in general by their loved ones, their adapting to a coach whose philosophy is different from theirs will be fairly easy. If athletes are in a sport for the artistic expression of an inner feeling (figure skating, for instance), they are less likely to compromise, and will most likely seek a new coach and training environment that are in harmony with their needs. If this skater is not attracted by rewards or trophies, then navigating such coaching obstacles will be easy. If recognition is yearned for then the athlete will either compromise or seek a more compatible coach.

Commitment is always difficult in the face of reality, and more specifically in relation to interpersonal limitations. Commitment, along with recommitment, is not so troublesome when people realize what they are up against and stand to gain or lose career-wise by following a particular course of action. Gains and losses are not always measured by the athlete's unconscious in terms of external rewards and opportunities; but oftentimes, by what holds one's damaged and evolving sense of self together.

Gains in self-esteem are extremely important motivators for athletes. Athletes, like all other people, need to feel that they have some control over their future and life circumstances — in short, their destiny. Normally, they experience this through their successes and achievements. When they set out to do something and accomplish it, this gives them a sense of mastery over self and life in general. They gain confidence to set goals and take risks because they believe they *can* succeed.

Reality is quite threatening; plans often go amiss because of societal trends, fluctuations within the culture, timing, personality conflicts, and, most typically, because of the fragility of people's identities. We are typically our own worst enemies, sabotaging our best chances for success. The deeper structures of our minds are so complex and elusive that we are constantly influenced, directed and crippled by old messages, fears, insecurities, and voracious needs to be appreciated, all of which have their origins in early family experiences and in a variety of traumas that have occurred in our lives. Our egos may be so scarred in ways that we are not aware of that we may never encounter them directly in the course of our lifetime. We only get clues of their existence as a result of our failures; these often fall into clear patterns if we are willing to take the time to look. We often fail to look because of the profundity of our defenses and the screens we have set up around ourselves in order to never have to experience that pain that accompanies frank appraisal of our distorted egos.

The sad and tragic aspect of this is that these scars do not disappear. They contribute to and influence us in ways that we have chosen not to acknowledge. When striving athletes encounter pressurized moments in their careers, these scars, or psychological weak points, begin to awaken and resonate with frightening demands. Depending on the severity of the stress in relation to these vulnerable points, athletes might choke, get sick, have a nervous breakdown, resort to drugs or alcohol, become depressed, lethargic or manic, overly aggressive, or, most typically, just lose interest in a sport that has consumed the major portion of their lives. There are a number of possible reactions depending on the situation and the meaning it has for the athlete's sense of self. Whatever the reaction, it will most likely be detrimental to the athlete's conscious intentions and actual performance. It will be negative for the sole reason that the athlete is reacting unconsciously to the situation. That is, he or she is not in control and will most likely be defensive and rigid. Stress leads to tension and tension leads to muscular contractions that prevent the athlete from being in a well practiced and optimal rhythm.

The old maxim "knowledge is power" is appropriate here. Knowing what your sport means to you, why you want and fear certain things so badly, will help you tremendously. Accordingly, one's directives — what needs to be given up and done in order to achieve one's goals — can be clearly envisioned. This is half the battle in sports. If athletes are clear as to who they are (especially in regard to personal limits, strengths and vulnerable spots), what they want and the price they will probably pay to get it, then usually much less will hinder them. Time limits, schedules for achieving success, and personalty conflicts will drop by the wayside of athletes in tune with themselves. These people are committed to their sport and remain so until they achieve their goals, no matter how long it takes. With such a mind-frame, the only ones who can stop athletes are themselves. They are willing to see their goals through to the end: What is begun is finished.

The above raises a very important concern. Why do most of us never really commit to anything? The answer simply is that it is too easy not to. All of us know that we live in a multifaceted society where options abound. We can, therefore, find a thousand and one reasons why we shouldn't commit to something, for example, a dream of being the best possible soccer player. Such a goal is usually framed in the following manner: My dream is to be a successful professional soccer player. The problem we all face, no matter how hard we try, is that there is no guarantee our dreams will pan out; consequently, I may dedicate my life to soccer and never play professional ball.

From one perspective, this is a personal tragedy; from the player's, he may feel he wasted his life. Our fictitious player could have married, gotten a better education, obtained a different job with a lucrative and secure future, socialized more, and so on. All of this was possible, but our player risked it all. As my colleague Richard Knowles once said, "The best you can do in terms of commitment is to be wholehearted and half sure." One can never read the future; this is the "kicker" that can paralyze us all.

The best people can do is to think through their goals, make the best possible decisions to realize them, and then follow through. Limited as we are, this is all we can do. We can never be positive of the outcome of anything.

The more aware people are of their motivation, the more unambivalent they will be. Lack of ambivalence allows athletes to have a stronger focus career-wise, and they will not be ashamed of their motives. Motivations are typically rooted in the unconscious because people find them incompatible with their self-perception. Athletes do not want to acknowledge them (for instance, being in sport solely for the money, or sexual contacts). Some athletes are also driven by the fact that they love to dominate and even injure their opponents. Society normally does not offer a space where people can get in touch with such primitive and aggressive impulses. As a result, most of us deceive ourselves in regard to them.

A great deal of subconscious conflict may go on, for example, with a football player who enjoys the brutal side of the sport. He may like to hurt people, but consciously knows that at some point others will not tolerate too much violence. He will usually repress this part of himself and either may be subconsciously ashamed of these impulses or may, on some occasion, unleash his violence in ways that are uncontrollable and destructive to his team and his own career. Who knows what Jack Tatum and George Atkinson of the now defunct Oakland Raiders struggled with emotionally because of their brutal style of play and the manner in which blood-thirsty fans reacted to their treatment of Lynn Swann, the Pittsburgh Steeler wide receiver who received at least two concussions at their hands. Football is based on violence, yet supposedly an athlete is expected to know the socially approved cut-off point for such aggressive acts. The fine line that separates a socially acceptable mode of expression and repression is very difficult to maintain, especially in the brutal arena of United States football. Many players must have a great deal of ambivalence.

The violent motives of pro football are less than Olympian, but they are true to life. If one is ashamed of such motives and cannot consciously accept them, these motives will develop a certain amount of autonomy in one's unconscious, providing quite a bit of torment and anxiety. The negative repercussions will come to light when the athlete is confronted with situations where people may take a dim view of his aggressive acts and true athletic motives. Coaches, owners and fans often give a player contradictory messages regarding the value of violence and sportsmanship in football.

Being upfront about the deeper motives within oneself is difficult, but gives the athlete a strong advantage. Athletes are less susceptible to being manipulated by issues dealing with and surrounding their motives, something dealt with more specifically in Chapter 8. If a football player is told that he is a "killer," a "mercenary," or a "player" (in the sexual sense) and is aware of the veracity of those labels, then he is not ashamed or taken off balance, whether these labels are true or not. He has come to terms with his reasons for being in the game, and does not have to deal with all the static around him. He knows that sports can provide him with an access to violence, money, and sex; he doesn't worry about what anyone accuses him of, and goes after what he wants. This athlete may be held in low repute in some sports circles, but in addition to being honest with himself and others, he is going to have a much clearer understanding of his motives, what the sport can provide for him, and what he hopes to achieve. His focus will be much more concentrated than if he was emotionally pulled in several directions.

Typically, athletes are immersed in a great deal of self-deception concerning their motives and commitments, and will usually be moody, guilt-ridden and therefore erratic in performance. Guilt will emerge when athletes catch a glimpse of their unconscious motives and find that they and possibly others consider such feelings abhorrent and incompatible with their conscious sense of who they *should* be. In these "shoulds," we get a strong echo of the many important people, especially parents, who have had such a strong role in shaping the athlete's orientation and motivation, the structure of his or her personality, manner of coping with life's challenges, and competitive style.

Similarly, if young athletes are aware that they need to be a star in order to feel good about themselves and that there is no guarantee that they will become one and that success might not happen at the rate and manner expected, then they are halfway toward their goals.

These athletes are willing to take the risks and are clear about what sport means to them. They know why they make all these sacrifices. If obstacles are encountered, they can reevaluate their strategies as to what they did or didn't do to get where they are now. For athletes, having genuine goals includes knowing what they are up against, why they are tackling a particular goal, and that success is not guaranteed. Doing this is not easy, because most people are caught up in an intricate web of self-deception. In the mobile and free society of the United States, where self-deception is a cultural phenomenon, the well-known or celebrity athlete has unlimited opportunities to avoid facing "the truths of life." A star can float from friend to friend, admirer to admirer, team to team, coach to coach. All this drifting helps him avoid that which is undermining his performance. This athlete can always find many well-wishers or bloodsuckers willing to help him maintain his self-deceptions. Others do this to reap their own rewards. These collusive pacts have to be mutually advantageous or they will not survive in the long run.

Another important factor of commitment is that athletes should be in a sport of their choosing, one that has individual meaning. Several rewards that attract and drive athletes are in the hands of others: coaches, general managers, judges, or university administrators. They hold the power to grant success, fame, even oblivion. If any of them do not like an athlete's particular style of play and approach to his or her sport, then the athlete can be discriminated against in regard to judging standards, or being benched or banned. Several track stars, especially in the field events (Dick Fosburg in the high jump), and Brian Oldfield (shot put and discus) have been discriminated against at different times in their careers because they challenged technical precedents. Athletes in every sport have met conservative, rigid, sports intelligentsia that have roadblocked or destroyed their careers because they refused to give up unique styles, which at the time were perceived as unorthodox and unacceptable. This happens most frequently in regard to athletes' personalities and temperaments. Unless you are a superstar like Reggie Jackson, it is very hard, in the world of competitive athletics, to be your own man. Most individuals are replaceable. The financial rewards of success are so exorbitant that athletes suppress their personalities in the service of those who can facilitate (or sometimes destroy) their careers. They know that there are 1,000 "hungry" athletes out there waiting to take their place.

Because so many of the tangible rewards of sport are in the hands of others, wanting them is a rather risky project. It is vital to realize that some people in power may not personally like an athlete or his style of play, perhaps because of jealousy. How is it possible to continue in the face of such opposition? A partial answer is that the athlete must find some kind of satisfaction or fulfillment in his daily training. Hard training in the hopes of some "pie in the sky" success is improbable. To continue on, athletes must find emotional nourishment in the game itself. They have to or they will burn themselves out and become frustrated with how long it takes to achieve their ultimate goals. There must be a sense of pleasure in the doing of the sport or the athlete will not find the stamina to weather the storms of adversity encountered along the way.

Most athletes are driven by the desire for money, notoriety, ego enhancement and the thrill of competition and victory. Any or all of these motives can be a driving force in the athlete's career, but it is the true athlete who receives daily support and nourishment from his sport that has a good chance at success. He is rewarded and sustained on a daily basis. The athlete after fame and money may have to wait indefinitely, and a lack of immediate gratification on some level usually burns him out and sends his dreams up in flames.

Immediate, daily satisfaction keeps athletes going after the larger economic rewards. They are aware every day what they need to put out and sacrifice to achieve their ultimate goals. This awareness drives them on.

Athletes longing for success must realize that it involves hard work and the sacrifices are great. Those who do realize it, if they have the physical skills and the proper attitude, will be hard to beat, and it will most likely be only a matter of time before they maximize their potential and possibly even achieve acclaim. These athletes make the necessary adjustments to ensure that they stay on the path toward individual goals. In this mind-frame, they may say to themselves. "If for whatever reasons I can't make it in this environment, with this coach, these players, and this style of play, then I will go to a new environment that is more in harmony with my style. Then I will become a success."

This move could mean a temporary setback, like redshirting for a year, a loss of salary or stardom, temporary anonymity, or having to move to a new city. It takes tremendous courage and a strong belief in one's self to make such a move. Many athletes, either out of fear or willful determination, stay with their original coaches or team placement and "go down with the ship."

An athlete who comes to mind in this context is Vince Ferragamo. He transferred from the University of California, after having to play behind Steve Bartkowski, redshirted one year, and was successful anew at the University of Nebraska. He took a big chance in making such a move. Despite his ultimate collegiate success, he was not pursued aggressively by the National Football League. He had a moderately successful career in the NFL, 1977–1980, taking the Los Angeles Rams to the Super Bowl. Again, he took another risk: He went to the Canadian Football League after a lengthy contract dispute and did quite poorly. Bucking the college system paid off for this very individualistic athlete, but he wasn't so fortunate with the pro's. By orthodox standards his route to the top was rather circuitous. What he achieved was primarily due to hard work and belief in himself.

Ultimately, motivation and commitment have to come from the athlete's heart. Despite having to compromise, athletes cannot give up their self sufficiency and the knowledge of what is best for themselves. They cannot let themselves be overly controlled by those in power (who believe that their way is the right and only way to do things).

The advent of the free-agent draft in baseball, player representatives, unions and bargaining agents have changed circumstances somewhat in professional sports. Leaving aside the question of their methods and ethics, it is quite evident that they have diffused the dictator-like influence of professional sports management. Athletes are now freer to control their destiny. Athletic servitude and indentured apprenticeships are now a thing of the past. Unfortunately, archaic and power-oriented systems still exist in abundance on the collegiate and high school levels. High school athletes are not allowed to go to schools that have programs most in tune with their psychological and athletic needs because of tax and competitive reasons.

Our concern, in addition to personal freedom and latitude, is to comprehend the nature of commitment, the ground from which the strongest and most durable commitments emerge. Athletes first and foremost have to be in tune with what is motivating them. They must be true to themselves, and at the same time try to adapt to their coaches' orientation and style. They will have to ultimately decide if they are being destroyed, both personally and professionally, by giving too much to their particular coach or program.

Players, because of the obvious risks, are usually afraid to jump ship. This could be a fatal mistake; they have probably given much time and energy to this coach or team. Changing now would mean going out into the unknown again, and the grass might not be greener on the other side. Perhaps by sticking it out a little longer, they will get what they want. This is a very serious and difficult decision.

If athletes stay in a static environment, disaster will happen in a matter of time. They will become passive-aggressive and depressed, have difficulty following coaching directives, or fail to put out 100 percent in training and competition. There will be little fulfillment in what they do, and athletics will become a grind. Performance in this climate will be affected negatively: In addition to athletes' reputation being severely damaged, they typically begin to lose confidence, and do not understand the emotional and psychological complexity of the situation that they are caught up in. They blindly live out the situation, their destinies controlled by their unconscious and how it deals with pressure.

Many players are traded or demand to be. These moves can either destroy or bolster a career, depending on the circumstances. Resulting success has to do with several factors. A new atmosphere won't guarantee improvement if athletes are beyond their prime; tired of their sport (burned out), lacking in motivation to continue; and leading personal lives that are seriously deteriorating. A move facilitates growth when athletes know that their styles would be more appreciated and utilized in a new environment. Being in the proper environment increases the chance of success, but is not a panacea for all that ails the athlete.

Making the right decision requires much forethought. Unfortunately, most athletes receive little counseling in this regard from their coaches, parents, and friends. Most people feel that athletes cannot be too choosy. I disagree; they usually have more choices and latitude than they imagine or even want to acknowledge, especially young athletes. They are ignorant of all the possibilities they have, and being unaware often is related to fear of change.

Every athlete is unique, with different personalities and emotional needs. Some need more public acclaim and playing time than others to feel good about themselves and to stay on top of their game. The choice of school is always a big decision that an aspiring professional athlete must consider. Part of the consideration is whether they have a chance to be a star—going to a small or non–NCAA school will increase the chances for this. Or, should they go to a school with a good reputation and the best competition, coaching, and players? Which will increase the chances of making the pros? If the athlete goes to a small school, he will be a big fish in a little pond. Statistics, reputation and confidence can be built. Pro scouts, however, may feel that athletes are untested against superior competition and it is therefore questionable if they can handle the pressure and competition of the professional ranks. This has proven to be a valid concern. Success, though, often breeds success; the more confident athletes are, the better they will perform and develop skills. Many, depending on their egos and temperaments, pass into obscurity because they chose a high-powered setting where they were lost in the shuffle, not getting a chance to polish their skills.

A large part of an athlete's battle is to find a supportive and productive environment. This requires good advice from parents, coaches, and possibly a professional, such as a sports psychologist. He or she, in conjunction with coaches and others, can come up with a true personality profile of the athlete based on style of play, ego needs, and temperament. If a data bank of different programs and settings from around the country were available, then athletes could check to see what they were qualified for, and which program their personal profile was compatible with. They could then make an intelligent decision as to where to go. This process, with the exception of a much-sought-after athlete, is nonexistent. Athletes typically decide on a program based more on externals (such as the name of the school) than on the internal constitution of its athletic program. Personality and style are often subordinated to the greedy intentions of seductive coaches little concerned about athletes' well-being and long-term career needs. Their program's chances of success are their primary consideration. The obvious ignorance and counterproductivity of this attitude are quite clear: Unhappy players are not productive.

These days of ignorance and neglect need to come to an end. The perpetuation of such ignorance results in an unnecessary and tragic waste of athletic potential and creativity. Athletes *need* to go where their skills are most appreciated and where they will develop maximally. Simultaneously, if coaches would choose athletes who fit their system the best, then both careers would be proportionally furthered.

No athlete can go on indefinitely without strong motivation and commitment. Both thrive on the progress that people make in respect to their goals. Progress is measured by success, partial or not. All athletes need to see the realization of certain tangible goals and rewards. Without these, especially at critical junctures in training, their motivation will recede and they will become less able to actualize their gifts. Without some sense of accomplishment and appreciation from important others, they will oftentimes end their careers long before their potential has been realized. This issue needs to be explored more closely.

Athletes might only be interested in a certain facet of their sport. A gymnast may love floor exercises and dislike such compulsories as the parallel bars, vaulting, or horse. A karate enthusiast may be primarily interested in self-defense, preparing him or herself for the brutality of the street. These athletes could encounter a variety of problems during the course of their training. The karate participator might hook up with a traditional teacher or school of martial arts. This school may believe in the "art" of karate, with street fighting being seen as a degradation and distortion of their ancient discipline. Athletes because of their orientation will run into a host of difficulties if they stay in this specific karate school. Many karate practitioners, because of ignorance, obstinacy, fear of failure and of quitting, stay in this disharmonious environment, become miserable and fail to develop. Their reasons for staying say much about the structure of their identity, and point to several psychological issues that are at its core. Passivity, guilt over perceived failure, dogged determination in the face of solid roadblocks, and fear of the unknown (Should I pull up stakes and go elsewhere?) say a great deal about self-structure and confidence.

In this example, the individual should have sought a karate school emphasizing self-defense and street survival. Several schools with this orientation are available. Here he would be in his proper environment, and would progress in rank, self-esteem, and physical prowess. He is the same athlete that he was in the other environment, with a critical difference. He feels at home, going with the flow rather than against it. The athlete knew what he wanted, looked for it, and had the courage to change. The move probably involved a step backward while he learned a new system and adapted to new personalities and training methods. This will most likely be temporary and not so difficult because the athlete's natural aptitudes and personal compatibility will allow him to quickly adapt to the new requirements. Personal needs and the demands of the new environment are now in harmony.

To stay in the old environment, the athlete would have continued to meet resistance from his seniors and failed to progress in rank. Worse, he most likely would have practiced the school's rank requirements in a half-hearted manner. This would decrease his chances of rank promotion and overall progression as a practitioner of self-defense. This contrary environment will either defeat him eventually, or at best, diminish his progress. Most athletes will wind up wasting valuable time and energy fighting the pressures and mentalities of others, energy that could be put to use in furthering their development.

Being in an environment characterized by friction, they will develop conscious *and* unconscious resentments toward those guiding their development. They will practice to perfection and excel in performance only when what they are doing matters to them and is appreciated by their peers. Preaching, threats, and exhortations will not reach the deepest levels of their motivation unless such promptings are in tune with what they really want and are of interest to them. Otherwise, athletes will perceive that most of what they are told to do is nonsense or politically motivated, and will do it just to please those who oversee them. At best, this will bring about behaviors that are rebellious, lackadaisical, passive-aggressive, or willfully determined to please. Any of these motivations are counterproductive, and probably destructive in the long run. This frame of mind is similar to riding a bicycle with the brakes on. The expenditure of energy will be dissipated by the friction and tension of not being in harmony with personal needs.

Few coaches know the mentalities of their players well enough to organize the orientation and style of their sport to fit their temperament. Athletes usually must adapt to the coach's personality and idiosyncracies. There are two options for young, impressionable and passive athletes: adapt or get lost. The ignorance of this approach is so obvious that it needs little description, but the question still remains, Why does this attitude of coaches continue to be played out with ever-increasing frequency?

The ignorance of coaches is protected because there are so many talented athletes in this country. Very few coaches and administrators have any idea or concern about what happens to athletes when they are cut from the team, or given little playing time, which causes disgust and eventually forces them to quit.

Typically when this happens life goes on. The athletes might be missed, temporarily, but they are the only ones who suffer. The reasons for their failure are ignored. Unless they have exceptional gifts such that a university or school could not do without their services, there is little concern for them. Most organizations and coaches fail to recognize that most athletes quit before their prime because they accept the judgment of a particular coach as final, instead of switching to an understanding and compatible environment.

Most people scoff at this idea. Athletics are competitive — as in the jungle, only the strong survive. At the same time, it is foolish not to allow athletes to develop all facets of their lives that will contribute to the improvement of their sport. This will facilitate athletes in making a strong contribution to their program, and allow them to develop their capabilities for survival, both in and out of the athletic world. The worst effect on athletes is that this negligence scars them psychologically the rest of their lives, a senseless tragedy that could have been averted with more knowledge of their psyches. Once upon a time, sports were designed to develop young people, rather than break them before their prime.

For sports to be a human and not just a money-making enterprise, athletes need to be treated with respect and dignity. They should be educated in order to understand themselves — specifically, how their minds work and affect their performance. They should also be made aware of their rights and the options they have as members of their teams, enabling them to make the best choices to ensure personal and athletic success. Educators, coaches, and university presidents must realize that we are in a very unique age. United States culture, because of its material wealth, has given the average citizen a great deal of leisure time and energy. For the first time in history, modern man is capable of pursuing a sport to its limits. Economic survival is no longer a fundamental drive for many people, meaning that the possibility of a career in athletics is a reality for them. The emphasis on sports both for athletes and the general public speaks to many issues of personal well-being and supervision that have never been of concern before, requiring a more thoughtful and honest approach.

As athletes mature, learn the ropes, and discover their options in the sports world, they will become less vulnerable to authoritative, insensitive, and ignorant authority figures. Many coaches have predetermined ideas of how the sport should be played, and do not take into consideration the individual natures of their athletes. By the time athletes become aware that they have joined an organization that is counter to their needs, their careers are typically in a tailspin or worse.

Athletes are continually exposed to options; among them are bucking the system, opposing precedent, getting off the well-trodden path. Training formats, schedules, environment, motivation and commitment all need to be in tune with athletes' talents, limits, and temperaments in order to be maximally efficient. Awareness of these necessities will transform athletes on all levels of their approach to and execution of sport. If their world is in tune with who they are, every aspect of athletics and life in general will benefit. If athletes work toward what they want in a way that at least approximates personal needs, there will be some personal fulfillment in everything they do. They will be less tense and more playful, and therefore creative, in respect to sport, especially in relation to the mechanical dimensions of training. Conditioning and tedious drills can become a source of joy and exhilaration. Athletes will do them because they know that their game will get better. Before, these drills may have been just the dictates of a mechanical and ignorant coach whom the player had a personality conflict with. Feeling free in an appreciative and supportive environment, athletes may feel safe enough to experiment with their game and develop new techniques and dimensions of their old style or approach. This is the environment in which athletes will push themselves to the apex of their abilities.

We have returned anew to an old issue: The more athletes are committed to their goals, the more relaxed and flexible they will be in regard to their actualization. They will eventually realize, in the face of the risks and lack of guarantees, that their commitment will be solid enough to withstand the many storms encountered. Athletes receive fulfillment knowing they are "going for it." This will sustain them in their quest and in the day-to-day grind. They know that improvement will be steady and continuous, and that their love of the game and belief in themselves are a match for any obstacles they might run into along the way. Athletes will practice their sport in a way that is true to themselves. They will be in pursuit of personal excellence, which involves the joyous realization that they are reaching for something they really want.

Sustained commitment to any one thing is rare, which frequently causes us to live with regret and self-reproach. This unfinished business gnaws at us and saps our vitality, making us feel that we can't cut it and that we have lost control over life. Frustrated athletes who didn't make it know this; their nocturnal dreams often call them back to those painful times when their careers hit the rocks. Seeing old buddies who either made it or who also fell off the path also stirs them up and causes a great deal of pain, continually undermines their belief in themselves and what they are able to accomplish, especially when attempting new careers or relationships. An ingrained fear of attempting new heights often becomes a lifelong companion.

Athletes' memories of failures often center around several deep-seated feelings of guilt and shame. Frequently they feel that they defeated themselves, played it safe, didn't sacrifice enough, didn't work on weak points, didn't try to adapt to their coaches' personalities and philosophies, and didn't modify short- and long-range goals; the list is endless. Unfortunately, hindsight always makes things clearer than when they are caught up in the moment, living out these dynamics instinctively. The bottom line is that athletes ultimately have no one to blame but themselves, and this is the hardest thing to accept. Success might have been possible if they had been stronger emotionally, giving them the necessary strength and discipline to meet the challenges encountered. This *might* becomes the gnawing doubt that if only things had been done differently, everything could have worked out.

Athletes need a second chance. Insight to analyze and meet present-day challenges during the growth of their careers needs to occur now and not in ten years when their careers are over.

Unmaterialized dreams and aspirations cannot be rationalized away. If athletes can truly say, "I gave it the best shot I could," then they succeeded. It might be difficult for their egos to acknowledge that even their best was not good enough to fulfill their dreams. This can be crushing to athletes, depending on the structure and strength of their identities. Despite not realizing personal goals, however, athletes will not have to live with the nagging guilt and self-doubt of "If only."

Immaturity, lack of foresight, rebelliousness, arrogance, or emotional instability, on the other hand, can mean the loss of a golden opportunity. Athletes in this category pay for this in one form or another for the remainder of their lives. The price also includes the possible loss of financial security, professional opportunities, and class status. Many athletes neglect their education out of laziness or folly, and when their careers end, they are at an economic level far below their potential.

Dedication to a goal means making certain choices, leaving other choices and possibilities behind, at least temporarily. There is no way to get everything at once; we are limited by our mentalities, personal constitution and resources, and the dictates of others. There is also only so much of the competitive pie to go around for those vying for top honors.

There are crucial crossroads in our lives where we have to make choices. Decisions to forsake economic rewards, lovers, or school in the name of sport are a high premium to pay. Many find the cost too high in the face of possible failure and the resulting loss of everything they have worked so hard for. Why some of us can forge forward in the face of these uncertainties while others cannot has been addressed in previous chapters; suffice it to say for now that winning and succeeding mean everything to certain individuals, and that they have nothing else in their lives if they do not succeed. One striking fact about the remarkable comeback of Pittsburgh Steelers running back Rocky Bleier was that after maiming his foot in Vietnam, he trained with almost fanatical determination to rehabilitate himself and reach a professional level of competence. In his book *Fighting Back* he stated that he was scared to death of failure and did not have any idea what to do with his life aside from football. His obsessive training and rehabilitation were that of a desperate man struggling for emotional and professional survival.

So many top-flight athletes emerge from the ghetto because theirs is a do-or-die situation. Sports are their way out and the means to reap the best of what society has to offer. Their motivation to succeed is at times reducible to survival. Athletes from middle- and upper-class families typically get bested by those from poor socio-economic backgrounds because they lack the killer instinct.

   Athletes dedicate themselves totally for a variety of reasons: fear, limited opportunities in other areas of life, an insatiable craving for money, success, and adulation, or love for the game and the intensity of competition. All these motivators can give athletes a chance to succeed; much of their success depends not only upon their natural physical gifts, but how badly they need to succeed.

   In this age of specialization, being good at something means that athletes have to dedicate their whole lives to it. Most of us have only so much natural ability and can therefore only be really good at one thing. Being at the top of the heap usually means total dedication. Why someone dedicates the whole of his or her life to the pursuit of one discipline or sport is a complicated question, and can only be answered by a careful study of the individual involved. Knowing, for instance, what Dan Gable's family was like could tell us a lot about his seemingly one dimensional life that centers around wrestling. He built himself up from a scrawny teenager through sheer hard work and will power to become a great amateur wrestler. He was a dominating Olympic champion and also the most successful wrestling coach in NCAA history. His University of Iowa teams won nine straight NCAA championships. He is legendary for being totally obsessed about wrestling and expecting his wrestlers to be also. His narrow focus has enabled him to be both one of history's elite wrestling practitioners and also the subject of great speculation in regard to the motivational structure of his personality.

   Many times, athletes themselves cannot say why they have dedicated themselves to their sport, while excluding the majority of all other life and career opportunities. Often, availability of resources has much to do with the choice of sport: Swimmers or surfers need to have water available, rugby players need to be in an area where rugby is played. Economics also plays a prime role in the choice of sport. Potentially gifted tennis players or dancers may end up playing baseball, basketball, or football because their parents could not afford the cost of lessons.

   Returning to commitment, it is quite clear that most of us do everything half-way. This is reasonable; we all need a balanced life to be personally fulfilled and to succeed. Athletes are human, and perform not only for reward and gain but also for personal happiness. Lonely and depressed athletes will have a slim chance of maximal performance. They might not even have the energy or desire to train hard if their personal lives are empty. They may see their training as absurd in view of the emptiness of their lives. (Why train so hard when one doesn't have the emotional essentials needed for inner contentment?) These athletes could be successful, but do not have someone to share their success with. Love is necessary for everyone, to varying degrees, depending on how much or little was received as children. Dedicated athletes perceive the sweat, pain and grind of training as being tedious and ridiculous if they are not content interpersonally. This is because they are continually sacrificing for something that is secondary to their emotional needs and at the same time precludes, even destroys, chances for interpersonal relationships.

Some athletes, conversely, realize the emptiness of their lives, and the only thing that gives them any sense of fulfillment is their sport. They throw themselves into it with redoubled effort to compensate for those dimensions that seem to be missing.

Even within the constraints of needing something (friendships, a mate, an education) to fall back on in case an athletic career does not pan out, most people still approach sport in a half-hearted manner. Some, depending on their natural physical endowments, may have to give up almost all other dimensions of life to succeed athletically. These people usually play it safe, possibly straining their relationships slightly because of the amount of time and energy that it takes to train and compete. They usually reap some degree of success in proportion to their sacrifices and their inherent gifts. It is usually a trade off—they keep their relationships, jobs, and education intact as they progress, pulling this whole fleet of interpersonal relations and responsibilities with them. This process is quite human. We all need, to varying degrees, a solid home front and personal life to function maximally. Yet some, because of psychological history, cannot risk giving up their support system to dedicate themselves wholeheartedly to their sport. These athletes usually fall by the wayside, are guilt-ridden and somehow realize that the unique constitution of their personalities got in the way of actualizing their dreams.

The ideal commitment, although very difficult to live out, involves total dedication. This means not being obsessed with sport and training every available minute to the exclusion of everything else. Such a willful and rigid approach is usually counterproductive and leads to emotional and physical burn out. Total dedication means that athletes are committed to their sport as they would be to a marriage partner. Whatever the problems, obstacles, or temporary setbacks, they will stick it out and see things to the end. Motivation goes beyond the particular moment. There is a life orientation and commitment with no time limit on the process. Athletes believe that they will get there and succeed no matter how long it takes.

To do this, athletes need to be consciously aware of what they are up against and drives them. All their dedication and sacrifice, or their attempt to fit sport into a well-rounded life, brings different advantages and disadvantages. Knowing how the scales balance for either alternative is crucial. Insight into these dynamics makes it very difficult for athletes to be self-deceptive, and harder to pass off failures onto other people or circumstances. Life circumstances and the influences of others will be accepted from the start as part of the game. These athletes will not be so naive as to believe that talent and performance are enough to secure success. The many snares laid out by greedy, jealous, hateful and political individuals could wipe out an athlete's career, but the informed athlete accepts these obstacles as a part of life and the whole athletic process.

Athletes rarely realize their dreams without encountering many obstacles. Obstacles and setbacks call for rededication, harder training, and the development of as much of their emotional and psychological selves as possible to actualize talents and realize goals. Knowledge of self, motivations, and the nature of their commitments will make people much more capable of handling strong resistance and crises that are a part of careers and personal lives. Many obstacles have the potential to knock people emotionally off balance, thus endangering their careers. When this happens, it is usually because they have not made strong commitments based on a clear understanding of themselves in relation to the demands of their sport. When choices are made in full view of the dynamics and facts of the situation, the deleterious influences of "sabotaging others" is reduced. Ambivalence and regret can be kept to a minimum, and success has more of a chance.

Obstacles and defeats alert committed athletes to what they must alter in terms of their mind sets. These are typically played out in regard to competitive and training strategies, the various personalities they encounter, timetables for realizing goals, diet, and living environments. Certain modifications and adaptations will put them back on the path to their goals. Now, athletes will have the added experience and knowledge that ensue from working through the hard times and failures. Psychologically unaware and weakly committed athletes will retire after encountering serious resistance. They will not have the courage, strength and endurance to go back to the drawing board. The magnitude and strength of their commitment are not enough to keep them afloat during these certain difficult times. Paltriness of commitment typically comes from entering athletics without people having clear comprehension of their deepest motives. These athletes typically sleep-walk through their lives and careers, unaware of the true nature and childhood origins of their motivations. This lack of insight breeds emotional ambivalence and therefore a lack of balance and integrity in their athletic drive to the top.

Commitment, again, involves recommitment. Its nature changes with time, and must be adapted to present circumstances and its relationship to future goals. No athletes reach their ultimate goals without encountering barriers that threaten to destroy all they have worked for. Their motives change not only as they mature, but as they either begin or fail to realize certain intermediate goals. For example, a martial artist may have initially taken up karate for self-defense. Once he learns how to defend himself, he must then question whether or not to continue training. The further he goes in training, the more he becomes attracted to the "artistic" dimensions of the discipline. The katas, or long dances, may become the focal part of his training. The concentration and technical excellence required to master these forms may become the new motivating force behind the athlete's approach and attitude towards his sport. The reasons for his training and the nature of his commitment have been altered. If he continues, he may ultimately be drawn to the spiritual core of the martial arts. His commitment has most likely continually changed and evolved throughout his career.

This process is not only in relation to his achievements, but most likely occurs in terms of his ego needs and fears. If he has dealt with these aspects of himself, he will be better prepared to realize and pursue the more profound dimensions of his art and personal makeup. He may have initially felt that if he could defend himself well, then he would feel more secure as a man. But, despite feeling safer in a fighting situation, he does not feel any more manly as he had anticipated or hoped. This is a valuable lesson, causing the martial artist to approach his art with a new emphasis and orientation. His commitment has been modified, based on his achievements in regard to his original intentions. Life forces people to learn and, one hopes, change. As a result, they could end up somewhere in their athletic evolution that they did not originally anticipate, but which they now realize is where they should be and probably even want to be.

Whatever aspect of sport is focused on — competitive, technical, or pleasurable — will have much to do with the approach people adopt. It will also say a great deal about who people are and what they are looking for in athletics, in terms of fulfilling something in their identities. Emotional stability and the chances of success depend on athletes' sense of self and goals. The standards used to measure success may be either personal or public.

The following chapter is an analysis of how athletes actually train, and specifically structure workouts in the pursuit of goals. Here we will see how motivation and commitment are played out in their training routines.

6
Training

An individual's psyche or mental state influences every aspect of his or her sport, right down to everyday training. An old fallacy still afloat in the sports world is that "practice makes perfect." Rote, or mechanical, practice is not enough, no matter how frequent. The aphorism should be rewritten to say, "*perfect* practice makes perfect." Unless athletes concentrate and have a particular goal in mind, their workouts will just be mechanical. For example, it is not enough for college-level high jumpers just to work on their jumps; they need to work on the weakest aspects of their jumping in order to improve. The former type of workout is a "maintenance workout." It just keeps the performance level at its current state. The athlete is really not trying to improve any one dimension, especially the weakest, of his or her jumping, but just jumping, with all the technical and attitudinal weaknesses still in place. It is really astounding how many athletes have workouts like these.

Most athletes have tremendous difficulty doing anything but maintenance workouts. They will get into shape, and therefore be stronger, if they train daily with intensity, even if the workouts are mechanical. Being stronger will definitely improve performance, but mechanical workouts will put it far below what it could be.

Every athlete knows this, but because of psychological barriers and the lack of proper advice, does not make the necessary corrections. Training routines need to be restructured in accordance with one's developing skills and the increasing demands of stronger competition. Routines have to be changed once they have been mastered, otherwise complacency develops. Boredom begins to color workouts, ability plateaus and motivation dwindles.

Depending on how long athletes are stuck on a particular training schedule, the competition may leave them in the dust. I know several runners who have done the same workouts for years. They run the same route at the same speed every day. They believe that because they are dedicated and consistent, they should be improving. Every time they have a less-than-flashy finish at a local 5- or 10K race, they return anew to their old training methods with intensified vigor. They are held back because they fail to mix in sprint workouts and interval training, change the distance of their normal route, and get into weights to develop their upper bodies. They have not stayed up with the "state of the art." We need to comprehend how their failure is possible, especially when many of them are intelligent professionals. It is of course the athletes' mental make up that leads them into this nonproductive trap.

Most coaches fail to see that athletes' resistance to change in their workout is often because they will seriously work on only those aspects of their game that they enjoy and believe in, and which keep them far away from feelings and conclusions they've drawn about certain experiences, people, themselves, and life in general. If they do not believe that a routine is effective, they will either consciously or unconsciously resist. They might go through the motions, even practice intently, but will not develop the skill properly because subconsciously they are at odds with themselves. These athletes are in conflict, practicing only to meet the demands of their coaches or some "ego ideal," not for themselves. With many, there is also a secret belief that they can succeed without practicing those underdeveloped portions of their game. Trying to "squeak by" is a very human fault, partly based on childlike fantasies and self deception.

Everyone feels relaxed and competent in a routine that is familiar and easily mastered. Ability to tolerate the anxiety that occurs when leaving the familiar and heading into the unknown has much to do with how athletes will progress. Such a move requires a strong sense of self. Going into the unknown is to deal with the unexpected, and there is no guarantee of how people will handle these unfamiliar demands or what repressed or immature parts of their personalities will be encountered. In addition to being confident and believing that the requirements of the new terrain can be handled, people must have a clear awareness of what their ultimate goals are. Knowing what needs to be done in order to realize certain ends is half the battle. Such awareness will push people through the difficult and awkward times that will be encountered when trying to master new skills. Since they know where they are going, there is a willingness to put up with the constant shakiness, even physical pain, of having to gain competence in less mature areas. The development of these new skills is seen minimally as an irritating digression and maximally as a waste of time (taking athletes away from their "real" practice). Athletes often equate real practice with what they can do "all out," as opposed to working on technique or form. Certain sports allow for such oversights, others do not. A lineman can lift weights most of the day and practice hard, whereas a dancer needs to work seriously on form in addition to cardiovascular conditioning, or he will be out of a job.

We still need to know why so many athletes fail to develop their full potential, and understand why so many train in a way that undermines, rather than facilitates, their chances of success. To answer these questions, we must go deeper into the psychology of athletes, specifically in regard to how they train.

One feeling that athletes must get used to is starting anew! Every stage of athletes' development requires new skills and strategies. To develop these, they must literally jump into training tasks that are by necessity slightly above their current levels of competence. They must accept, at least initially, that they will feel awkward and easily fatigued, almost like an incompetent child. The conclusion is stark: When one aspect of training is mastered, new aspects or regimes must become the new goal. Likewise, if a training routine is not producing the desired effects, then the focus must be changed.

It is very difficult (and scary) for adults after the age of 18 to begin anything new, whether it is a sport, musical instrument or art form. They have spent their whole lives trying to outgrow feelings of clumsiness, embarrassment and shame that frequently accompanied their fledgling attempts at new behaviors and tasks. To complicate this, children are extremely jealous of the fact that adults can do things much better than they can. They long for the day when they can be "cool," sophisticated, facile, and most of all, competent. Depending on their home environment and earlier coaches, childrens' youthful attempts at mastery could have been a source of ridicule. If so, they received an indelible message: Being a beginner is a source of shame. In some cases, an entire athletic career may be dedicated to proving a person is not klutzy. Self protection becomes the overriding theme of these athletes' lives. They may never again put themselves in a position of being a beginner and being perceived as inadequate or second-class citizens. Many adult athletes carry this image with them their whole lives; this deep-rooted fear causes much anxiety when a situation is encountered requiring the abandonment of their old way of doing things. This threatens their sense of identity. All athletes have a great deal of personal investment and self-worth tied up in what they can and cannot do, which is the result of psychic and emotional scars from the past. These usually center around certain strong messages they received from their parents as to what kind of persons they *should* and *should not* be. Specific to our concerns here is that many athletes feel that they should *never* be awkward or incompetent, even temporarily. For them, every encounter, with new demands placed on their current skills and level of competence, will automatically influence them to balk at the "new frontiers." The degree of hesitancy will be in relation to the depth of their past personal insecurities and emotional scars.

All athletes encounter physical plateaus in their calisthenics or weight-training programs. For example, an athlete has steadily progressed and discovers that he can do twelve repetitions of 60 pounds on the curl machine. Now, according to his program, he needs to raise the weight to 70 pounds. At 80 pounds, however, it becomes work again — eight repetitions at this weight require all his strength and determination. Here he has hit his first serious limit; all increases up to this weight were handled relatively easily. He feels awkward and frustrated, perhaps inadequate, facing his limits. Many athletes, for instance, balk at a particular weight. It is just too hard, with too much pain and too many feelings of impatience involved. All who train with weights hate these magical barriers they can't seem to get beyond. It may take months to go from 180 to 200 pounds on the bench press. Frustration leads to frustration, and finally one may have to drop down to a lower weight with more frequent repetitions again. At that level the athlete may feel competent and secure again. Yet he may hate that 200 pounds; it controlled him and made him feel like a "wimp," a child again because he just could not lift it.

The athlete will eventually have to abandon his or her routine and work on muscle groupings that complement the chest, or primary, muscles for bench pressing. Tricep and upper-back exercises will help to eventually overcome the 200-pound barrier. The hardest part will be making the switch to the new regime. The athlete may feel defeated and taken off his game plan, not sure if this complementary program would get him over the 200-pound mark. The athlete may resent the fact that, unlike a "real man," he couldn't just plow straight ahead (with will power and grit) to achieve his goals. Despite not liking the delay, or the feeling that he had to take a circuitous route to get where he wanted to go, he must alter his routine. Most male athletes want to feel like those "he men" who can muscle their way through these tough "limit" situations. This attitude said much about an athlete's mentality and personality, as well as his developmental influences.

Reaching new heights requires rededication and reformulation of training routines. Why do so many find it difficult to leave the known and mastered behind? Do new goals require more energy, dedication and output? Possibly, but the answer is not so simple. The more relevant question is, What does the work *mean* to the athlete?

Does it signify that he or she is only an average athlete, if extra hard work is needed to achieve things? Perhaps I am inferior, the athlete thinks, with little natural talent to be a star. The message for some athletes is that too much work signifies lack of talent and inferiority. This may or may not be the reality, but it represents something very significant to those who never had to work and struggle for success. People who have been told that they are just average have probably had it conveyed to them in a way that makes them ashamed of themselves. The issue of "work" hits upon a very sensitive and painful issue for these athletes. Some might not have encountered their limits until later in life. Being unfamiliar with this situation could put their identities through many changes they are psychologically unprepared for. Most people experienced these trials at an earlier time in life and found them very unnerving.

Practice routines for athletes are often not geared to developing the full scope of their abilities, a common occurrence of great interest to a sports psychologist. Why don't athletes practice what they need to in order to excel? Many will often continue working on what they are good at, overdeveloping skills they are already proficient in, and neglecting their weakest components.

We see this everyday in professional baseball and basketball players who do not work seriously on drills to develop their defensive skills. There could be a variety of psychological reasons for this. Athletes might feel that they get very little acclaim for being a great defensive player. Those who hit .300 or score 20 points a game get all the glory. Depending on his psychological makeup, an athlete may subconsciously resist practicing something that he may feel is not in line with his best interest and aspirations. This could be felt on a personal as well as professional level (he may not like the "image" of being known as a defensive player). An aversion to this could have its roots back in the playground days of grammar school. His memory may contain the message that the celebrities were the offensive stars, and the average players were the ones who picked up the scraps and played tough defense. For many, in addition, defense is decidedly less elating than offense. Most importantly, many psychologically vulnerable or obsessive athletes may feel that when they are practicing defensive skills, they are taking precious time and energy away from what is important in their game — their offensive repertoire. They feel that this is their strength, and there is some factual basis to this feeling. It is quite rare that a basketball or baseball player makes it to the pros based on defensive skills only. This athlete's rationale is that if he does not keep his offensive skills in tune, then they will deteriorate. For him, neglecting his offensive skills is like watching a skyscraper he has built gradually tumble and fall, a quite ludicrous situation.

An important dimension of training is drive, or motivation. Some question why they are forced to do certain exercises and drills when they can see little or no benefit. If forced to do so, they may feel that their autonomy as intelligent persons is being insulted. This could cause athletes to resent those who are making them do the drills, resulting in personality conflicts. As stated earlier, immature athletes could become passive-aggressive in relation to the demands and routines expected of them by coaches, and end up getting little or no benefit out of the exercises they design. Likewise, athletes may feel held down by exercises they feel are more beneficial to the less developed and competent athletes. Finally, there are those who thrive on and are energized by competition; they come alive in front of an opponent or audience. They are listless and apathetic during practice, and feel that it is unrealistic and not challenging enough. It is essential to be aware of these individual differences and how they point to different psychological issues that motivate and structure athletes' attitudes and actual preparation for their sport.

All this speaks to aspects of people's sense of self and the effects and impressions made by important others on them throughout the course of their lives. These issues and others fundamentally influence and color how athletes progress, succeed or fail, and attempt to develop themselves through training. Many influences shape their mentality and structure the content of their athletic careers. Those not attuned to the issues mentioned in this chapter are a living tragedy. They are sabotaging their careers at the same time they think they are consciously trying to further their athletic pursuits.

All the issues that can subvert training are typically subconscious. Athletes are unaware of them, and more importantly, the power of the psychological conflicts these issues are concrete manifestations of, and how they can pull them down midway through their careers. Ignorance is not bliss; it typically means tragedy and failure for an athlete. All athletes need to become aware of their deeper motivations and the constitution of their identities. Without this knowledge, they are doomed to be controlled and misdirected by personal fears and motivations that are at the center of their personalities and self-esteem.

There are many things athletes must do to grow and develop and keep up with every improving competition. They need the necessary physical skills, but must also be psychologically mature and aware. Mature athletes will be able to go beyond the *source* of

the demands that certain coaches place on them putting the problem into perspective. The content of the demand to do certain drills
and exercises will be looked at objectively in terms of what is ultimately best for the athlete. Those who have a problem or a personality conflict with a coach tend to dismiss out of hand much of
what he prescribes, simply because they resent this individual.
Consequently, the value of the coach's suggestions falls on deaf
ears regardless of the validity of the advice.

Mature athletes always know what the personal risks and advantages are in regard to whatever they are doing. They are
realistic enough to know that bucking the system is going to cost
something, and usually comes down to the question of whether or
not the gains outweigh the minuses. Those who know their
ultimate goals will make the right career decisions, and keep in full
view why they do a particular training procedure. Most importantly, they know why new forms of training, more in tune with
the state of their proficiency and less to fortify or support a damaged or fragile ego, need to be introduced.

For instance, some athletes yearn for fame, wealth, and public
acclaim. Their main motivation is to climb the ladder to the top,
unless they have extraordinary talent (in view of their goals), it
would be foolish for them to buck the system too much, because
they have too much to lose. They can not afford to alienate their
coach, manager, or team owners — they have too much power over
them. They can bench, suspend, trade, ban, redshirt, or force
athletes to transfer, or even exert enough pressure to force them to
quit altogether. Consequently, the intensity and demands of high-
level athletics in the United States require that for athletes to be
successful, they must know who they are, what they want and must
do both interpersonally and preparatorily (training-wise) in order
to actualize their goals.

There are others who are into a sport for more personal reasons. They have more individualistic and deeply personal motives
for participating than the average and less sensitive individual, and
tend to "run alone." They have a vision of how they should experience their sport. All competitive athletes want to be recognized
by the public, but this is not the most pressing concern for some.
There is a long list of illustrious athletes who broke with conven-
tional coaching and training practices and went their own way.

Dick Fosburg's "Fosburg flop" revolutioned the art of high jumping Dwight Stones, another phenomenal high jumper, claims to
have literally trained on his own (went without a coach) during the
height of his career. Gene Tunney, Jack Johnson and Muhammad
Ali brought new stylistic innovations to boxing that were not initially well-received. Their usage of footwork, counterattack, and
training methods revolutionized the sport. Toller Cranston and
others have made figure skating a vehicle for avant-garde and ex-
pressive dance on ice. Similarly, Bruce Lee revolutionized the martial arts not only be teaching non–Orientals, but by dispensing with
the archaic forms and techniques that were appropriate to feudal
Asia but not American streets. His June-Keet Do style of karate
was a radical break with traditional Asian practices and allowed
him to express his personal vision of karate, and provided him with
the framework in which he could continue to rededicate and maximize the utilization of his God-given gifts (intellectual, spiritual
and physical). If he did not have the courage to go his own way
(design his own unique training methods), he may have quit karate
out of boredom and frustration, or would have conformed to a
more traditional system which was far too restrictive. This would
have diminished his growth as a practitioner.

The athletes mentioned above definitely bucked the system
and still succeeded. There is no guarantee that people will succeed
if they remain true to their own vision of how to train and approach their sport, but it is definitely possible to be true to your
style and needs and still succeed. On the other hand, there are thou-
sands who have bucked the system and ended up in obscurity. Every athlete, therefore, has to decide where the proper balance between conformity and self-expression is.

Athletes must be clear on where they are going, and in tune
with their emotional needs. Most importantly, they need to get in
tune with their subconscious motivations (many of which are part
of their sense of self and self esteem). This will allow them to devise
a method of training that is in harmony with their goals, one which
they can live with wholeheartedly, and one which leads to acceptance that much of what they do is essential to their futures. In this
way, they can be at peace with themselves and others. Ultimately,
mature athletes will come to know what their goals and idiosyn-
cratic approaches to sport are, and what the need to feel emo-

tionally fulfilled. With this in mind, they will place themselves in training environments where their energy is not wasted by getting caught up in differences of opinion over training methods. They will be where they belong and are appreciated.

In this way, athletes can get down to the business at hand, which is to train and ultimately realize their dreams, and not get caught up in the mire of antithetical viewpoints and personalities. This will give them a much greater return on their investment of time and energy, with fewer internal and external conflicts to distract them. This frame of mind can only enhance a career. Simply put, if athletes do not train intensely and constantly improve their game, they will typically find an early and often unrequested retirement.

7
Failure

This chapter deals with what is behind athletes' failures, both on the playing field and with their careers. There is a particular kind of athlete that this book is not specifically concerned with — those that develop their potential but come up short just because they don't have the God-given talent to go any further. They are not failures, no matter how far they objectively go in their careers. Theirs are the real success stories: They pushed to the limit and got as much out of themselves as they could. Very few people can boast of that!

There is another type we will focus on: Those with the tremendous potential and physical talent who fail or quit way before their potential is ever actualized. These athletes often have superior mental or physical skills, yet are often vanquished by an inferior opponent, especially in highly pressurized situations. The worlds of boxing and tennis, for example, are filled with personalities of this sort. We need to understand how this happens and how gifted athletes torpedo their own careers.

Ideally, although few athletes are emotionally strong enough to take such a stance, failure is educational. When they fail, they are alerted to specific blind spots in their training methods, inadequate dimensions of their actual performance and strategy, and eating and sleeping habits prior to an event. All of these come together to help produce a particular performance by athletes. Failure does not just refer to losing a contest. It can also refer to subpar performance, a failure in a much more personal and less objective sense. In a certain way, anything less than the best people are capable of at this moment can be considered a failure.

Failure basically alerts us to what went wrong and what we are not doing correctly in preparation. Depending on the degree of failure and its context (for example, a national championship), it will be harder for athletes to analyze the whole situation objectively and learn from it. In most cases, when an athlete believes that he has trained as hard as possible for an event and still comes up short, his attitude, typically, is "What is the use in continuing? My best just isn't good enough." In reality, it is extremely rare for athletes to perform optimally. They may have done their best on the day of the event, but the preparation might have been less than optimal. Most do not want to acknowledge this fact. It means that they have to own up to the fact that they were ignorant, or cut corners, in their preparations.

More importantly though, depending on their life circumstances (familial, financial, and educational), they may be unable to compete again no matter what the level. It is heartbreaking to know that one trained all his life for the opportunity to compete in the Olympics, but failure here would mean financial and emotional pressures so great that trying again would not be possible. In some sports, athletes may be benched, traded, or retired because of poor performance, thus making it that much more difficult to take personal responsibility for the defeat. Lack of talent in this case is not the deciding factor in the defeat. Athletes' personality dimensions are: mental blocks, psychic scars, and ambivalent motivation. These combine to produce inadequate training and preparation on all levels of life, including practice, diet, sleep, and interpersonal relationships. It is difficult to admit after defeat that one trained improperly. Many athletes know during their daily workouts that they should be working on other facets of their game, but for reasons stated in the last chapter, continue to do what they are best at (maintenance workouts). In many cases, athletes are simply defeated by a superior opponent. This is something outside their control. Within their grasp, however, is the ability to prepare themselves so that they can do the best they are capable of at this time.

We need to understand how an athlete like Bruce Jenner, who at 19 years of age placed far off the mark in the decathlon event in the 1972 Olympics in Munich, but was able to come back four years later and win the gold medal in the same event in the Montreal Olympics. His performance there also set a world record. Was it just because he was only 19 years old and competed in Munich on a lark? It is possible that he realized he was young and had not fully matured as a decathlon practitioner. He could have seen Munich as a learning experience and realized that with time, he could be better. Yet, the cold fact is he had the psychological flexibility and stability to put his Munich performance into proper perspective, looking at it and seeing what he needed to do in order to win the event in 1976. The real test would have been to see, if he had failed in 1976, whether he learned from his mistakes and went on to 1980. A sixth-place finish in 1976 would have been a marked improvement over his 1972 performance, meaning he had learned and improved a great deal. It is quite possible that four more years of the same intense training could produce a win in the 1980 decathlon. There are many "ifs" that can enter into the space of four more years after a serious disappointment. To continue training for four more years would take much discipline, sacrifice and hard work, especially for a 10-event athlete. It is now known how much Jenner and his wife, Christy, gave up in those years between 1972 and 1976. I doubt if either of them could have gone on for another four; their eventual divorce probably had its roots in this difficult and sacrificing time.

There are so many athletes who fail to win an event or reach a level of competence at a specific time and thus begin a decline that ultimately leads to giving up. Something snaps in the minds of those who do not get what they believe they deserve at a certain time. It is very hard to maintain an intense focus and high degree of sacrifice over a period of time with such a loss. The desire to train diligently is lost. These individuals who have the hardest time recovering from setbacks are usually the ones who look to their sportive success to fill in the gaps in their damaged egos.

People need certain essential rewards or benefits in order for them to go on in life. Financial security and strong love relationships are all very important to everyone's well being. People who fail to fulfill these basic needs of life will not continue to pour time, energy and income into something that does not provide them with these essentials, just as no one dying of thirst will pour water onto sand. All athletes must decide if their potential has "maxed out" and they are at the end of the developmental line.

Something that distinguishes athletes from the rest of the population is that they are typically individuals who want to better themselves, at least in regard to their sport. They are always looking for an "edge," constantly searching for new training techniques, exercises, nutritional information, or weight-training equipment that will help them get the most out of their natural endowments. As a result of modern technology, science, and coaching techniques, athletes have many alternatives to choose from in order to strengthen their game. Totally dedicated athletes, such as discus-thrower Al Oerter, have utilized just about every modern device, including computers, to analyze their technique in the search for excellence. At age 45, standing 6'5" and weighing 245 pounds, he is a living testament to ultimate dedication (20 years at the top of his sport, four Olympic gold medals in the discus). He is also supremely focused and mentally strong. Mr. Oerter has undoubtedly had to face severe pressures and crises in his life, which are clearly related to his "one-point focus" on discus throwing. Something had to give somewhere; most likely it was in the area of his interpersonal relationships. Al Oerter is an excellent example of an athlete who has dug deeply and come up with the best he is capable of. His success is clearly fueled by his obsession for excellence, but as he passed his prime, every passing year demanded a more total commitment to make up for the effects of aging. He is an example of an athlete who either lived up to his potential or forged and pushed his potential to its limits. Only he knows what such sacrifices cost him in other aspects of his life.

Sadly, most athletes quit before they begin to face the limits of their potential. This fact often has its roots not only in the realities of having to make a living, but more specifically in the psychological composition of the athlete's mind. What holds many athletes' identities together is their need for success. Many can be thrown into an identity crisis (they do not know who they are, what they are capable of, or what their self-worth is) if they fail in relation to some strongly desired goal. Very few who are dedicated and have structured their lives in the pursuit of their athletic goals can postpone success indefinitely. Their identities are primarily invested in the sport; it is, for many, the only thing that they feel good at, justifying their self-worth and existence in general. Their fear is that important people in their lives will ignore or berate them if they fail, and their value in respect to others will greatly diminish. Many athletes are terrified, most typically subconsciously, by the prospect that they will not know who they are, what they should do with their lives and possibly even be abandoned by others whom they need, if they do not live up to certain athletic expectations.

These people suffer greatly, but typically in an unconscious manner. They feel that they are unworthy of love for being themselves without their athletic accomplishments. This is a serious dilemma: Athletes begin to realize on some level that success, especially in the past, will not guarantee once and for all their much needed feelings of self-affirmation. Renewed success, at best, only keeps their fragile feelings of self-worth temporarily afloat. Success keeps the athlete from sinking into shame, guilt, feelings of unworthiness and of being unlovable. The fear is that others only give to them and want to be near them because of their success. These people typically come from families that give a certain variety of love specifically for successful performance. Their success often bolstered their parents' sense of worth. Having such successful children obviously casts a positive light on the parents, and many look to their children to bolster their status in the community. If children are good and successful, then the parents must be also good parents and successful people. Many parents follow this kind of faulty logic. Children with such parents learn at an early age that failure can lead to their parents' being disappointed, withdrawing their love and affection accordingly. Emotional survival therefore depends on success.

As mentioned earlier, children who receive messages equating love and performance usually have them indelibly printed on their minds. They are driven athletes who find little fulfillment in their successes, and cannot enjoy them because they must always be looking to the future for the next opportunity to succeed or fail. Hence they are always ahead of themselves and rarely take the time or feel comfortable enough to enjoy their victories. They are usually in the sport for the wrong reasons; burning themselves out and being devastated by failure. Failure must be avoided at all costs. Athletes with this mind frame are not flexible and joyous enough to be able to take failures in stride. Failure for them is the equivalent of emotional annihilation.

Athletes in this fearful position will be shaky and driven, feeling that they must always "be" at their sport. Time wasted just increases the chances of failure, meaning that time not spent training or more typically spent worrying obsessively over training is perceived as time squandered. Training will be compulsive and therefore mechanical, joyless and most often out of touch with those areas of their game that need improvement. Training protects the status quo (those aspects that they are already good at, rather than working on those that would increase *overall* performance). For these reasons, failure or subpar performance is often a consequence of the athletes' mental state. It often dictates how they prepare themselves for competition — either properly or most often improperly.

Similarly, the state of athletes' private lives will greatly influence their ability to train and compete at the maximum level. If their parents or mates are opposed to their success, or drive them to it, then much of their personal support system or avenues of reinforcement will be contingent upon their accomplishments. At first athletes drive themselves to meet the needs of those who hold the strings on their self-esteem. They will eventually, at least subconsciously, rebel at having to sell themselves out in order to be loved. Neurotic athletes will eventually become passive-aggressive (or subconsciously resist) and begin to fail in order to test and displease those who say they love them. Athletes, on some level of awareness, will realize that the love they receive is dependent upon a self-image they may want, but which at the same time they live up to only to curry the affections of others. They will resent the fact that it is not they who are loved, but the benefits that others receive because of their achievements. Parents or mates may bask in the limelight of their fame and recognition; eventually, within this atmosphere, training and performance must suffer.

The danger once again is that the *full scope* of the resentment of having to sell themselves to be loved is typically unconscious.

Passive-aggressive or rebellious behavior is neurotic because it is an indirect form of communication that alienates others and damages athletes' performance and relationships. If they were consciously aware of this, the need for sports psychology would be negligible and athletes could directly confront themselves and others. Likewise they could evaluate their motives for being in the sport at all. These reflections, based on all relevant information, would put athletes in a position to make the choices and decisions that are best for them inside *and* outside the realm of sports.

Why does losing a game, or athletes' placement on a ranking continuum, cause disruption? Why, when failing to achieve what they worked so hard for, do they fold? Why is it that when a child fails to make a Little League team, he may never compete in baseball again, or if another athlete fails to get a scholarship to college, he may never compete seriously again? Conversely, some adolescents will go to small or junior colleges or even make major college teams as "walk-ons"! Similarly, why do some athletes have an unspectacular year and retire altogether, whereas others who are less gifted but who have great desire have a mediocre year and as a result become determined to train harder? These individuals may get on a serious weight-training program in the off season in order to compensate for their lack of physical strength, but the gifted athletes may quit after a poor season, or more typically continue to compete but never with the tenacity and energy that they are capable of. Some of these athletes loved, or still love, the game, but, something is amiss. It is not always the athlete with the most talent who makes it to the top. Determination, discipline and "heart" have so much to do with ultimate success. These intangible qualities are part and parcel of the personality and psyche of the athlete. The mind and structure of athletes' identities fuel, sustain, and drive them toward the actualization of their gifts. This area of focus is often badly neglected, even abused, by coaches and others of what might be called the sports intelligentsia. Coaches, parents and others are often guilty of damaging athletes' identities irreparably by playing "head" games" with them because of their own personal fears and jealousies. A person's mentality, at critical times in his development, is highly vulnerable to the judgments of others. The negative effects of these interactions can neutralize (depending on their severity) even the most divinely endowed physical capacities of the athlete.

Some athletes fail because they do not feel (subconsciously) that it is proper for them to succeed because they aren't good enough or especially deserving enough to succeed. The latter feeling has its roots in messages they have received from others over the years to the effect that they are "bad kids," so labelled because they failed to conform to the dictates of domineering parents, coaches, or teachers. Their lack of passivity is a threat to those around them. These threatened individuals often feel that they have to pull the kids down a notch or take some "steam out of their engines." These messages have a tremendous effect; telling athletes that they are selfish, arrogant, and most poignantly unloveable can have the effect of totally undermining their approach to sport, especially when success seems to be a real possibility. Success will only confirm in their and others' minds that they are haughty and different from those around them. This, coupled with being different and coming from an unsupportive or jealous environment, means being shunned and alienated from a valued group. Success, then, becomes something subconsciously to be avoided. On the other hand, if athletes are not cut off because of their success, others could expect or demand it of them to accomplish even greater feats. This kind of pressure can emotionally paralyze an athlete and influence him or her to settle for mediocrity.

Those involved in sports who have authority and power over the lives and formative influences that so strongly affect children's sense of self and confidence must become more attuned to how their sense of identity, fears, insecurities, and ego needs lie at the base of their performance. A good example of this is as follows: I went to high school with a number of talented basketball players whose careers ended there largely because of a particularly unstable coach. Some of them never played organized basketball again. The pain of having to deal with this coach undermined many of the young men's sense of confidence and fair play and their ideal of the meaning of sports. This experience left such a bitter taste in their mouths that many of them never competed athletically again in any sport. Unfortunately, they were young, naive, idealistic and psychologically unsophisticated, and had no idea of the extent of the coach's pathology or the complexity of human interaction.

Being unable to put the whole experience into perspective, they just personalized it. They felt that something was wrong with them, and were not good enough to excel at this point in their lives. All they knew was that they were either not playing or not playing well for this coach. The cold reality they felt was that they failed. They may have cursed the coach and realized that he was too demanding and extremely irrational, but in the final analysis they shouldered the burden of their personal and their team's demise. They were not emotionally stable enough to learn from the experience and go on. At this formative time in their lives they were seriously damaged. High school is an extremely critical time for young athletes; adolescence itself is a time of complex changes and personal uncertainty. Without some degree of success and guidance, it becomes very difficult for athletes to muster the courage and motivation to head on to higher competition at the university level.

These athletes were getting too strong a dosage of reality, and were not mature enough to handle and grow from it. They were butting up against an insecure and authoritative individual who had a lot of power over their athletic careers. It was simple: If they did not get along with the coach's disturbed ways they didn't play, and their chances of playing college ball were nil. The dream of all of these players was to play college ball. Along with their youth and inexperience, unfortunately, was that they were all in a situation that was over their heads. They were not in a position of equality, for coaches at this private, all-boys' school held all the strings.

For many reasons, none of the school administrators were aware of what was going on until it was too late. The students had courage and pride and didn't complain to their parents or teachers. They downplayed everything they said about the coach. Parents or teachers could not believe that a high school basketball coach was making his players do combat and knock-down drills 60 percent of the time. Additionally, he gave strict orders that no one could, at any time, shoot outside of the key. Players were constantly getting hurt because of his insane drills, and parents and administrators, for their own reasons, were not getting involved. During my four-year stint there, four to six talented players a year were emotionally damaged or never played basketball again. The simple explanation for their career demise was that they received no help, guidance, or supervision from adults who could have alleviated the situation. Some probably said, "That's the breaks. Life is like that. One has to deal with people like him at all levels." This could be true, but it is not always absolutely necessary and people (especially in the case of children) can and should do something about it.

Every team, from the pros down to the peewee leagues, should have at least one individual, representing the league, who investigates coaching practices and the effects they have on athletes. There should be some forum for players to discuss how they are being treated. Coaches have too much power and can damage many young athletes because of a lack of compassion and understanding of what athletes (and people in general) need to flourish personally and athletically. Those who supervise how players are being handled need not be professional psychologists, social workers, or counselors, although their services would probably make for an ideal situation. They simply need to be intelligent, reflective and sensitive, and attuned to the potential damage that can result from coaches who are either disturbed or who stress winning to the exclusion of personal development.

I am not advocating a Pollyannish world for competitive athletes. I know that the bottom line of all athletics is winning and its relation to the almighty dollar. Winning provides fortunes for universities, professional owners and coaches. Players also benefit tremendously from having winning seasons. Even on the lowest levels of amateur athletics, winning provides ego reinforcement for players and coaches. Further lucrative opportunities in the coaching profession largely rest on a coach's win–loss record.

Even within this monetary framework, which is the name of the game in the United States, coaches could get more out of their players if they took the time and energy to know who their players are, what they are up against psychologically, and what this sport means to their future and their personal sense of self. Good business sense dictates knowing who your personnel are and what they are personally dealing with. Coaches, parents and administrators do not need access to their psychological profiles and personal histories; this is none of their business. They *should* be attuned to the individual differences of each of their players and know in some fashion where these differences come from and what they personally need to perform at their peak at that time.

Additionally, supervisors of coaches must be sensitized to the possibility of wasted talent. It is obvious when athletes compete far below their potential, and the reason is usually reducible to a few factors. They could be ambivalent or in conflict about their sport due to family and personal influences or their relationship to their coach. Whatever the cause, a sensitive and inquiring adult should be able to easily gauge the primary dynamics of the situation. Remedies, depending on the extent of the problem, are usually simple if dialogue and communication are facilitated and encouraged by those involved. Let us return to the issue of motivation and its relationship to failure.

If persons in authority can understand why athletes compete and train, they are halfway toward coaching them properly and keeping their progress on the forward edge. If an athlete's motivation is clear in his mind, his failures or subpar performances are perceived, no matter how painfully, as temporary setbacks.

Someone fixing his car illustrates this point. In fixing a car, one typically makes several mistakes at first, especially when attempting something for the first time, like gapping the points. Normally one keeps trying and learning each time he gaps the points, eventually getting it correct. There is usually very little shame in having to make many trials unless one is under the watchful gaze of a disapproving adult or employer. In fact, if we did not learn from our mistakes, we would never get it correct and would have to pay someone to fix our cars.

Why is it so difficult for us to take the same relaxed attitude in respect to our own athletic mistakes? Obviously the situation is quite different. Athletically we are continually being judged and evaluated by others as to how many points we score, what our batting average is, what our rank in karate is, and so forth. Athletes are on public display and others are judging their worth from within their value systems. Also these same coaches and judges, along with athletes' friends and family, often tend to determine (based on performance) their athletic and personal worth. A case in point is as follows.

In the final seconds of the 1982 NCAA Division I-A men's basketball championship game, Georgetown University's Fred Brown mistakenly threw the ball to James Worthy, a University of

North Carolina player near his own goal, with Georgetown down by one point, resulting in a Tar Heel victory. The pass was a give-away, the type that players have nightmares about. The guy choked, at the most crucial point in the most important game of the year in front of the whole country. Brown had a great year otherwise, but many dimensions of his personal life must have suf-fered as a result of that errant pass. His relationships on campus — with women, friends, and teammates — must have been shaken. As we can see from this, the higher the stakes, the greater the penalties are for failure. These liabilities are not just in terms of material benefits but also in relationship to one's feelings of self-worth in and out of the world of athletics. Fred Brown was lucky enough to have a coach like John Thompson. His integrity and maturity allowed Brown to put the event into perspective and eventually into the past. A more unstable coach could have laid such a head trip on Brown that he might never have been heard from again. He came back the next year to contribute significantly to Georgetown's championship season.

Failure many times hits at the core of one's identity. It is at these times that an athlete is most susceptible to ruin. Very few boxers who have been knocked out have the raw courage and psy-chological fortitude to go back into the ring with renewed inten-sity, especially with the fighter who delivered the blow. With fight-ers we are discussing very high stakes (permanent brain damage and possibly the loss of their lives). Many would say, perhaps cor-rectly, that such a fighter should not get in the ring under any cir-cumstances again. The point is that through such a crushing failure and trauma a great deal can be learned if the athlete has the moti-vation to come back. Joe Frazier against Muhammad Ali and Sugar Ray Leonard against Roberto Duran are two excellent ex-amples of fighters who suffered vicious losses and were able to rise from the ashes and eventually come back to defeat their op-ponents. Leonard learned that he could not stand toe to toe with Duran and slug it out as he had done in their first fight. Leonard had obviously wanted to show the boxing world in his first fight with Duran that he was tough and a slugger in addition to being a skillful boxer. He was able to accept his limits as well as his talents (that he was one of the fastest and most stylistic fighters of all time), and use them to defeat Duran, a boxing legend.

It is a typical scenario in football and basketball that top-flight teams get beaten by inferior opponents. The loss usually jolts them out of their complacency and alerts them to what they need to strengthen in order to win consistently and avoid such losses in the future. This is an invaluable lesson. Many intelligent coaches, when perceiving that their players are resting on their laurels, will purposely not prepare them properly for a tough game early in the season in the hopes that they will lose. A defeat at this time is not going to ruin their season and will provide a tremendous learning opportunity for the complacent players. The lesson can be easily absorbed because the price of the loss is not so debilitating. Of more concern is the price athletes pay for losing or failure at critical junctures in their careers. Here the cost is often to their identities and their chances of continuing on in the sport. Timing and perspective are critical components of dealing properly with failure.

Failure within a proper attitudinal posture is instructive. Unfortunately, failure is often devastating. Positively, it can attune athletes to the realities, risks, and fine points of their athletic style, all of which need to be recognized and tuned up for chances of success in the future to be increased. If athletes can acknowledge their mistakes there is no way that they cannot improve athletically — this is inevitable. Failure at crucial times, however, can be very wounding, especially when athletes have very little insight into what the meaning of failure is to their sense of self and how subconsciously they contributed to setting up the failure by ascribing certain meanings to it that increased the probability of its occurrence.

The full meaning of failure rarely becomes clear to athletes only after years have elapsed. This is unfortunate, because if athletes could analyze the *perceived* failure in the present, they could use such knowledge to bolster and fortify their careers before it is too late. Gaining insight into the experience years later does little for anyone's career and feelings of confidence. Just imagine if knowledge gained from hindsight could be used in the present. If athletes realize that they may never have another chance to be a league champion, or even to compete again, they might go at the event with a "never say die" intensity. That comes from knowing that this and all of life are only once-in-a-lifetime opportunities.

The hurtful effects of failure can be circumvented and turned to positive advantage if athletes (especially with the help of a competent sports psychologist) can bring into conscious awareness the many meanings and issues that are stirred up by a particular failure or setback. These, unless properly handled, can potentially put a career to rest. The tragedy is that athletes often quit at a time when they are closest to realizing their aspirations. Many times, with just a little fine tuning, they can get back on the upward track, but premature retirement usually occurs because of their sense of frustration and inadequacy. Such feelings typically have their roots in unconscious dimensions of their personalities. The impetus for a rebirth of a career can come from being aware of the multitude of images, painful conclusions, old messages, judgments and central conflicts that undermine our most conscientious and concerted efforts.

8

The Psych Out and the Choke

People's sense of identity and personal history influence so
many areas of their athletic careers: which sport they choose, how
they train and, most importantly, how they perform. The next
chapters will show that athletes' psychological makeup is the foundation out of which they are able to utilize their physical gifts and
skills to handle the pressure of a competitive situation.

Why do athletes, even the best, "choke"? To answer this, we
need to know how choking is grounded in the specific meanings
that the competitive situation has for one's sense of self, and how
these meanings negatively influence performance. Answering the
question, Why do athletes choke? goes right to the heart of sports
psychology and all its complexities.

Psychological pressures, whether they are head games played
with others or just crippling feelings of anxiety, find a receptive
and vulnerable spot within athletes' sense of self. This pressure
often hits all the weak links in the chain of issues that come
together in a unique fashion to make up their identities and interpersonal lives. Here are some common examples: An amateur
boxer is to face a fighter that he has never seen before. His opponent is bigger, stronger, more muscular, quicker, and looks

meaner. Any or all of the opponent's perceived attributes could objectively be clear advantages in the ring, but none, singularly or combined, can guarantee victory. Of importance is how these characteristics are perceived by the amateur in the ring. Any that are perceived as an advantage, whether based on reality or not, will definitely have a psychological effect on our fighter and therefore become an advantage for his opponent. This will definitely weaken our boxer's chance of success because he is immediately "psyched out," or fighting from a defensive posture.

Similarly, pole vaulters prance, careen, stretch, and flip in their warm-ups. This is part of the competitive dance, the psych out. Movement, quickness, muscularity, and flexibility are decided advantages in this event, but none guarantees victory on any particular day. How high off the ground the bar is when the athlete goes over is the name of the game. Even the splendid albatross looks like a klutz on dry land, but once airborne it is majestic. These observations in the case of the boxer and the pole vaulter reach deep within an insecure athlete's mind and call up self doubt.

Many basketball players watching opposing players warm up are often intimidated beyond belief. Observing their opponents hit 25-foot jump shots with ease or do "whirlybird" dunks with the grace of gazelles in flight can unnerve anyone. The only thing that matters, however, is who wins the game, not the slickness of warm-ups. Many veterans of competitive athletics know that practice and the "real thing" are two different realities. Bruce Lee expressed this point precisely in the film *Enter the Dragon*. He faces an opponent who is very vicious looking, six inches taller and at least 50 pounds heavier. Prior to the bout, Lee's opponent throws a board in the air and breaks it with a reverse punch right in front of Lee's face. Lee calmly responds in a way that sums it all up when he states, "Boards don't hit back." The point is obvious: One can do wonders in practice, but facing a skilled, crafty and determined opponent is another story. Here there is no guarantee of victory. No matter how many advantages one may seem to have over an opponent, the latter's skill level can never be gauged on external observations.

There are objective measures to determine if one athlete is better than the next: size, strength, quickness, agility, and hand-eye coordination. Why are some athletes demoralized when they perceive these advantages in others, whereas others' composure and confidence are unaffected? The answer once again lies in the athletes' feelings of self-confidence, motives for competing and overall determination in the face of adversity. All these find their roots stretching all the way back to childhood and even infancy, and are an inherent part of the athletes' self-image.

Sports journals give very little attention to the psychological head games that many athletes in competitive situations play with one another. Two of the most famous "psych out" artists of modern times were Muhammad Ali and Mark Spitz; they were also tremendously physically gifted and dedicated.

Throughout his career, Ali developed a myriad of tactics in and out of the ring that threw his opponents mentally off balance. His poems, aphorisms, prefight jibes at Sonny Liston, George Foreman, Floyd Patterson and Joe Frazier are now classics. He continually taunted Liston, called him "the bear" and appeared on his front lawn in the middle of the night prior to their bout and demanded they fight right then, instead of in their scheduled bout. These were all mind games, and this confident belligerence had an effect on Liston. Ali's confidence about the certainty of Liston's demise clearly could shake the most confident of fighters, as it did Liston. This analysis presumes that the fight between Ali and Liston was not fixed. It would have been quite difficult for Liston to transcend the self-doubt that would have normally occurred in a situation where a young, inexperienced fighter showed no fear of the heavyweight champion of the world, who had the reputation of being brutal and having survived several years in prison. Ali brought much anxiety into Liston's life.

Another of Ali's famous tactics was the development of the "rope-a-dope" technique. Ali used this on George Foreman in the tropical heat of Zaire, Africa. After six rounds of covering up and letting Foreman unload his best shots (all the while verbally taunting Foreman that he had no power), Ali had Foreman psyched out and exhausted. By round seven, Foreman was "punched out," both physically and mentally, because he felt that his best shots did not phase Ali. This emotionally devastated Foreman; he felt impotent and became a sitting duck for Ali in round seven. Ali then proceeded to demolish him at will. Foreman didn't last long and was never himself after that fight.

Mark Spitz was much more subtle in his employment of the psych out. Many swimmers who competed against Spitz in the 1968 Olympics said that his seven gold medals were a fluke, feeling that he did not earn them honestly. They accused him of "head tripping" and of constantly playing mind games with his fellow competitors. Athletes who bite the psychological bait will always demean those who offer it. Their views are based on the idea that all athletes should be forthright and gentlemanly, that is, aboveboard. Whether Spitz's antics were cheap or street-wise is not the issue. The issue is that his accusers took no responsibility for swallowing the bait he offered hook, line and sinker.

Spitz performed many psychological maneuvers during the Olympic games, including arriving very late for the warm-ups preceding his events. Obviously, most athletes were very nervous before an Olympic race. Swimmers opposing Spitz were jarred to see him arrive late and appear cool, calm and collected. Spitz's actions and attitude conveyed this very powerful message: I am so confident about winning that I don't even need to warm up. Spitz would also tell those swimmers that he had sized up as psychologically vulnerable that he was going to "eat them up" and probably wouldn't even have to "put it into full gear" to beat them. This was usually done in the locker room before the race.

The effect of such tactics would be negligible if it were not for the structure of the listener's identity. The psych out can take an almost infinite number of forms. It can touch one's physical limitations (one is too little, fat, weak, or slow). Also, many taunts are directed at poor past performances. Baseball players notoriously receive "cat calls" for bad plays they have made in the past. These jeers touch on many insecurities. For some players not being perfect in all their physical attributes and successful in all past pursuits makes them feel inadequate. These feelings could result in their quitting so as to not risk further embarrassment. These antics have been a part of baseball for decades. A player's inadequate fielding and hitting are all considered fair game for hecklers. Baseball players are rarely allowed to forget when they choked in a big game.

Athletes are continually teased and taunted, even by their own teammates. These caustic comments are expressed for several reasons: jealousy, repressed anger, fears of intimacy, or strategy (to throw him or her off balance).

The results of actual performances are what athletes utilize to build their feelings of self-worth. The vulnerable spot of all athletes' identities is failing (the inability to accept or overcome personal limitations, inadequacies, poor past performances, and especially choking). All athletes have self-doubt. They wonder whether they are capable of handling the stress and competition of this event or that opponent. No athlete or team is invincible. Even if they have won every time to date, there is no guarantee that they will win tomorrow. The intermediate hurdler Edwin Moses is a case in point. Having won 106 straight races is still no guarantee that he will win his next race. Most athletes are fully aware of their weak points, and all can be beaten if the timing and situation are right. Defeat usually finds its origins and first foothold in the mind. Athletes who can be mentally shaken are usually halfway to being beaten in the actual physical competition.

Self-doubt is the key. There is not a single human being who does not have doubts about his or her capacity to accomplish certain things. All people have physical, emotional and psychological limitations; for some this realization is a source of embarrassment and leads to feelings of personal inadequacy. For others, the acceptance of their limitations is a source of strength. Most people know they are limited but still try to accomplish their goals.

These psychologically vulnerable areas of identity at times reach all the way to the base of athletes' mentalities. They point to their sense of who they are and should be (a winner, loser, "real man," "flighty little girl," a woman who must be equal to a man, and so on). Just as important, these feelings refer to who these people are in the eyes of those who love them, and who they love, respect, need, *and* hate (those who have ridiculed, given up on, or stigmatized them in the past). Most psychological anxiety centers around those who have withheld the needed love and respect people need to feel good about themselves. This throws people emotionally off balance, and they perceive themselves to be "no good" emotionally and athletically. Athletes will typically feel that they can never do anything right in a situation where the outcome will be critically evaluated by important others. Futility sets in; they feel that no matter what they do, they can never please those people judging them (parents, lovers, competitors, and coaches). Athletes may feel they have been branded as inferior and unlovable, causing their anxiety level to increase whenever they are in the others' presence. They stiffen up, become self-conscious, and end up performing in a defensive posture. Their minds are on their critics' negative perception of them, not on the event at hand. Athletes will typically lose their concentration and perform badly, thus reinforcing their critical audience's negative perception. This cycle unfortunately repeats itself again and again.

The verbal barbs from competitors can point to fears of choking, pain and injury, looking bad, and embarrassment. These feelings are typically subconscious, and speak to athletes' perceptions of who they must be in order to earn feelings of self-acceptance, respect, and ultimately love. Likewise, the feelings of anxiety that arise in regard to vulnerable points speak to who athletes must not be. Becoming the kind of person that is intolerable to oneself (a choker, for example) speaks to a person's fears of losing his or her self respect, and more importantly, the love of others. The cruel fact of life is that people usually love someone only when that person lives up to their personal expectations. In view of the above, relaxation exercises are often cosmetic and fail to deal with what is making the athlete anxious in the first place.

Many, because of the messages they received about themselves from their parents, feel that they are not good enough to deserve affection and love just for being themselves. Their style (way of doing things) is simply not adequate; the other's is always right. To receive attention and approval, the task must be performed their way. Any time people are in a situation where they do not measure up, it hurts them terribly, and undermines their feelings of self because it confirms what others may have communicated to them for years and about which they have had their own suspicions as well. "Average" in this environment has the connotation of being unimportant, passed over, or ignored. This means that people are seen as unworthy of respect, care, love, and affection. Competition for these athletes is both terrifying and compulsively needed. They need athletic success like a junkie needs a fix. Success in their minds is the only thing that gives them a semblance of value, respect, and ability in the eyes of others. These athletes are obviously in a very vulnerable position. They will most likely be choice prey for those skilled at head games.

The power, influence, and impact that the core of one's

psychological makeup plays in actual performance cannot be stressed enough. The power of psychological influences in sports is tremendous. How others attempt to knock athletes off balance depends on how experienced athletes are in the psychological warfare of competitive athletics. If athletes are emotionally stable, much of the motivation that drives them has been worked through maturely and consciously chosen. These integrations determine how well athletes handle the stresses, strains and uncertainties of competitive athletics.

How true athletes are to their needs and aspirations has much to do with how they handle big-time pressure. An athlete whose "head is on straight" and participates in his sport for the right reasons has a better chance to succeed. This takes time and maturity, and there is much emotional homework to do to get to this place. Ideally, through experience and learning, athletes will take up their sport primarily for themselves and not to please others. Psychologically healthy athletes need to prove their self-worth only to themselves.

The amount of psychological insight that athletes have into who they are, and what pushes them will influence how well they handle stressful situations. A cardinal rule in psychology is that the more aware and accepting people are of certain deep-rooted feelings, the less they can be influenced and manipulated by others in regard to those feelings.

Most people, even though the everyday world is competitive, do not have to put their egos and talents on the line the way a competitive athlete does. Where concrete performance is the measure of athletes, anything that has a powerful influence on performance must be recognized and either controlled or adapted to by them. If something is essential to their sense of self and continues to remain unconscious, they will be manipulated by external circumstances and influences and the unacceptable (and repressed) parts of their personalities. If athletes can integrate their repressed fears, desires, and needs into their conscious selves, the locus of control for their actions and ability to perform will emanate from within, and will therefore cease to find its control and power in the hands of others.

The psych out is the amount of meaning and import people give to certain statements or actions which undermine their sense of who they are and what they are capable of at a particular moment in time. Vulnerability to the psych out contributes to the athlete's inability to develop a unitary, unfettered presence to the athletic task at hand, whether training or actual competition.

People can be knocked off balance by the slightest comment at vulnerable times in their lives. Bodybuilders often destroy an opponent's confidence with stinging remarks about his or her physique. For example, a bodybuilder has naturally skinny calves. Everybody, including judges, has told him for years that his "placings" have been largely due to his skinny calves, making him somewhat self-conscious about them. He decides to build up his calves for the next year's Mr. Universe competition, and trains diligently. Just before going on stage for the contest, his two most formidable challengers say at different times that he looks great but that he should try not to let those skinny calves show too much!

The issue for this athlete is how well he knows himself, and how objective he can be. In his case, one of three things is true: His calves have developed somewhat but they are still skinny; his competitors are trying to psych him out; in reality his calves have developed considerably. The first two possibilities speak to his personal limitations — naturally skinny calves. Can he put this into perspective and not blow it out of proportion? Perhaps the rest of his physique is marvelous, but no bodybuilder is free of flaws. The object of his sport is to eliminate them, but some bodybuilders, for psychological reasons, have great difficulty in accepting their limits and are quite vulnerable in this regard. A mature individual knows, without outside feedback, whether his calves are developed or not. Accepting whether they are or are not skinny puts him in control and makes it impossible for others to shake his confidence.

Returning to the example of the amateur boxer, suppose he ends up in the ring with a bigger, stronger, and possibly more skillful opponent. He has three options: to fight, not fight, or go through the motions. Many boxers take the last alternative. Fighting outright may mean injury, not fighting would be seen as an act of cowardness within the value system of a very macho sport, and going through the motions is to play both sides against the middle. The fighter does not get hurt or labeled a coward. The problem here is that he gives away his self-respect and possibly a golden opportunity to grow and advance his career. If the opponent is so overwhelmingly superior, he should be smart enough not to get into the ring in the first place. But this is not the case in this example: The disadvantage lies primarily in the mind of the intimidated athlete. He is giving the other an advantage which in reality does not exist.

The psychologically strong athlete will say, "If I am here and have to fight (which is my choice), my best alternative is to fight to the maximum of my ability. This gives me the best chance of not being hurt, of retaining my self respect, of not embarrassing myself, and of possibly winning." In this sense the objective outcome (winning or losing) is secondary to knowing that he did his best. This is really the only criterion that an athlete can judge himself by. Everything else lies in the hands of the judges or how good he and his competitor are on a given day. The only thing within the athlete's power is the maximal effort that he can produce during the contest. If he has trained improperly, or is overmatched or unprepared physically or mentally, he will pay a price. At the least it will be a learning experience; the best possible scenario has him digging deeply within himself to find energy and talents that he has not been willing to utilize under more ideal and less trying circumstances. This is not advocating macho foolhardiness. No fighter should enter a contest of any kind, for any of the reasons mentioned previously, if it is obvious that he will be seriously or permanently injured.

An athlete should place himself in a position where the odds are high that he will *not* incur serious injury to his body or feelings of self-confidence. Doing so would be downright stupid. A boxer must always insure that he will be able to continue on in his quest for excellence. There are exceptions, especially when the stakes are high or the athlete is in a situation like the Olympics in which he has trained all of his life and it may be more appropriate to push himself to the point of serious but not permanent injury. At these times there is no tomorrow. For some the Olympics may be the culmination of an athletic career.

Psychology is the key to understanding athletic performance. Another example from karate illustrates this point. Physical violence is a dominating factor with karate, and exposes practitioners to great psychological stress. The higher the stakes (i.e., risk of permanent injury), the greater the chance that the athletes' fears, anxieties and insecurities will emerge.

A trained karate fighter familiar with the mental dimensions of fighting has an excellent sense of his opponent from the moment he first stands and faces him. The determination, fearlessness, and calmness in his physical bearing tell his opponent much about what he is up against. A skillful fighter senses immediately if his opponent is scared or intimidated, and knows that if he can get his opponent on the "backpedal" (defensive) at the commencement of the fight, the battle is half over. The first serious exchange can decide the direction of the match. One fighter may take the other's best shot and deflect it, showing no ill effects, while at the same time inflicting serious damage with his counterpunch. This encounter can shake a person's confidence: Events happen so quickly and hit emotionally on many levels at once. There is little time to analyze how he is reacting emotionally. Preparatory work is paramount, and the value of psychological insight or awareness of what one is capable of cannot be underplayed.

One exchange doesn't mean anything for the psychologically strong fighter. Momentum often swings several times in a fight, and a psychological observer needs to comprehend how these occur. One fighter usually intimidates or hurts the other and therefore feels in control. The other could think at this time that he is out of control, but is still not beaten, so he goes after his opponent while he still has the energy. It all boils down to one fighter feeling his power and capacity to dominate in the moment, therefore taking control of the situation. Inability to take control of a situation is mainly due to lack of confidence. The superior athlete knows that he has an excellent chance of winning under any circumstances, no matter who the opponent is or how the fight is going at a particular moment. The other fighter will have to beat him; he is not going to defeat himself through self-doubt and nervousness. The superior fighter, no matter the opponent, starts out strong, and has the ability to defeat him from the outset.

Not all athletes need therapy or the aid of a sports psychologist to be on top of their game. Self-awareness into the head games, manipulative tactics, and ego needs of those whom athletes encounter along their personal and athletic evolution will help increase their chances of success.

The relationship between athletes' self awareness and their perception of important people (competitors, coaches, enemies, or former and current lovers) is a dimension of performance that is typically unexplored by the sports intelligentsia. Important issues are often missed when only champion athletes are analyzed. Because they have reached the top, it is assumed that all has gone smoothly for them. Sometimes this is true, but there are many who fall by the wayside that are living examples of how an imbalanced mentality reacts and is overcome by the severe pressures of personal life, lack of self-esteem, and competitive athletics.

Many who reach the top of their sport had to encounter and overcome several personal and emotional crises in their lives. These are usually jarring encounters with personal limits, coaches, and painful messages from important people in their past. Successful athletes are not protected from these obstacles; they must deal with them like all other people. The resolution of these issues allows them to proceed further in their careers because each encounter offers a greater susceptibility to failure but also a unique opportunity to grow stronger and become more stable by meeting and conquering these crises.

The number of athletes crushed by the complexity of psychological pressures connected with athletics is a tragedy. It is mind boggling to reflect upon how long and hard serious athletes train and then realize that the majority fail. They fail because they lack the insight to realize that their own worst enemy is themselves, and their mentalities. Their personality structure also dissolves and undoes all that they have worked so hard to achieve.

The moral of this is similar to the Greek myth of Sisyphus. Sisyphus, a legendary King of Corinth, was condemned to push a large stone up to the top of a high mountain, only to have it fall back down again, for eternity. Athletes do not need to inflict on themselves the same fate as Sisyphus'. After they have transcended many personal obstacles, they do not need to watch in disbelief as their efforts to reach higher ground only result in their ending up closer to the bottom than they were years before. These are alternatives: all athletes have the power, through self understanding, to keep going forward in the face of adversity and not to lose what they have worked so hard for. This will be discussed in the last chapter.

Ideally, when athletes perform, they should be doing just that, but there is usually a large discrepancy between the ideal and real. Humans are very complicated, and are influenced by many dimensions of their being that they are not aware of. Even conscious reflections during competition can cause anxiety and disturb their concentration and weaken performance.

Having good and bad days is typically accepted in sports circles, but superior athletes are not *necessarily* defeated on a bad day. Because of their psychological integrity and strength, they can find a little something extra that will push them over the top, even under the worst of circumstances. Despite their psychological complexities, athletes spend very little time trying to comprehend themselves and how their mentalities either positively or negatively affect their performances. Understanding this helps them realize their fullest potential. Psychological components of personality need to be brought out in the open, analyzed, and used as an ally rather than as a most destructive opponent.

The motivational structure of athletes' subconscious minds, specifically that which was designed in their formative years growing up in the family, attunes them in certain contexts to not only what is possible but also how these possibilities will or will not affirm the personas they were raised to believe they must be. These false selves were adopted to obtain the love and respect of those around them, became internalized and thus became the modi operandi for all actions, both athletic and nonathletic.

Unfortunately, the idealized selves are not who they really are. The real selves have been squashed in the service of getting approval from their parents, who had definite ideas about what kind of people they should be. The created self or ego had little to do with the unique qualities and personality of the individual, as previously analyzed. This ideal self carries with it a whole complex of shoulds. As a result the athlete is constantly under pressure to meet severe standards of excellence *and* highly specific behavioral directives.

These athletes are walking time bombs, ready to self-destruct when some situation, demand or person touches a weak link in their prefabricated, unsubstantial selves. Their false selves are held together by psychic chicken wire and thus live in constant dread of being exposed for what they are—fakes.

Not having personalities rooted in their souls and in their

unique qualities, they are in actuality vulnerable to a multitude of threats with very few ways to defend against them. These come in waves in the form of all the "psych outs" athletes encounter.

The reader can now begin to understand why athletes so often experience stress and the accompanying physical tension which throw them out of their well-practiced rhythms. These are the most common reasons why athletes fail, and are more responsible than any other factors for athletes not reaching their potential.

Being unaware of, and subconsciously trying to live out an idealized version of a self shaped through years of parental influence is the single most important factor in the failure to develop the appropriate levels of skill, conditioning and performance that would be a true reflection of the athlete's innate capacity and years of concerted practice. There are few opponents more skilled, crafty, and capable of defeating him than his own subconscious.

The next chapter deals with optimal performance, the ultimate goal for all pursuing a career in athletics. This topic will be approached from a new and unexplored dimension of sport. The psychological arena will be the site of much future athletic training. As physical and technical components of athletic research and development reach their limits, the psychological or mental aspects of athletes will be the deciding factor in distinguishing champions from the competent and also-rans. Optimal performance comes from a clear understanding of what people hope to accomplish. With this knowledge, athletes can enter practice or actual competition psychologically balanced, enabling them to focus all of their energy on performance.

9
Ultimate Performance

The ultimate that athletes can aspire to is the actualization of their potential. This is a more difficult goal than winning for a very simple reason: Very gifted athletes may reach such heights, but might use only 90 percent of their talent to get there. They were never challenged and forced to develop their potential totally, meaning they had no desire to utilize the remaining 10 percent. Understandably, the most any athlete can accomplish may be solely in terms of his or her personal battle to perform optimally. Some drive themselves because they are objective enough to know that their chances of success lie primarily in developing themselves to the limit, but the average person only fantasizes about doing this, relying on dreams to live these aspirations out.

There are several ways to talk about optimal performance. One is as something way off in the future that will come at the pinnacle of a career. Here athletes, after a lifetime of training and dedication, reach the apex of their abilities with a personal best that could be a world record. Every coach and serious spectator has watched innumerable athletes struggle to develop their talents. Somewhere along the line they peak, reaching the height of their capacity to perform. This may or may not be the maximum of

131

what they are capable of, but it could be as far as they will go. The test of an athlete's development may be measured in a single event or on a particular day of competition where he may perform at a level that he will never be able to duplicate again. This is one kind of optimal performance, but its occurrence is too rare to have any real and meaningful impact on the athlete's growth. There is another type of optimal performance which is much closer to home. At any moment, whether in practice, conditioning, or actual competition, the athlete strives to give 100 percent of what he is capable of, at that *particular* point in time.

Giving 100 percent to anything is nearly impossible, but is the upper limit that all athletes strive for. This, in some sports, could be equated with passing out (distance runners), and possible death (boxers). It is rarely appropriate to put forth such an effort except perhaps in a life or death situation. The point is that athletes' performances rarely get anywhere near 100 effort.

Optimal performance is also related to what people are capable of on a particular day. They may transcend tiredness, injury, a level of competition, fear, or depression. Conditions are rarely perfect, and when called on to perform, athletes usually have a plethora of reasons why they cannot do something to the best of their ability. These excuses are usually fairly plausible (too cold, hot, tired, sore, etc.). Ghetto athletes, on the other hand, demonstrate that they understand perfectly the reality of life. The bottom line for them is "put up or shut up." Either the challenge is met or not. Excuses do not matter because once the event is over, second chances are only wishful thinking.

Several questions emerge: Can I free myself up enough to put out 100 percent of what I am capable? Can I commit my whole body and mind to this one event? Can I let go of my feelings of sickness, depression, anger, hurt, or exhaustion, particularly in the eyes of important others? Can I be free of worry that I may embarrass or humiliate myself, or be thought of as a showboat, or a wimp? If athletes can let go of these images then something exciting can happen; they can be totally "in their situation." They will react appropriately to the continually changing demands of any competitive moment and instinctively anticipate them, thus keeping one step ahead of certain shifts and changes.

Athletes occasionally go into a trance-like state where nothing seems to go wrong. Bernard King, playing for the New York Knicks in the 1984 National Basketball Association quarterfinals, was averaging 40 points a game. In one game he was awesome, and seemed to be playing unconsciously. He was tossing in 25 footers with three men climbing all over him without even looking at the basket. King was definitely on that night. Dwight Clark and Joe Montana of the 1982 Super Bowl Champion San Francisco 49ers are another example of athletes totally letting go of psychological fears and worries and getting into the flow of the moment.

Toward the end of the 1982 season, Clark and Montana seemed to be magically connected. Passes would be thrown and caught that defied explanation. At times Montana would throw the ball and it was obvious that he could not see Clark; likewise, Clark would make catches that should not have been made. Whatever the reasons for the oustanding performances of King, Clark and Montana, something was definitely different. They seemed to be in another dimension. Getting to this kind of unique space obviously is not easy and is quite uncommon, but these three were free of any internal and external disturbances that could possibly interfere with the expression of their highly refined abilities. They are an example of individuals totally absorbed with what they were doing, performing in a manner almost beyond their abilities.

King, Montana, and Clark had to let go of petty concerns that could have pulled them down. At that time, their one reason for existence was to perform; everything else was secondary. Their emotional hurts, pains, and worries were left behind, and no one could play any mind games with them.

More realistically, athletes will most often not break any records on any particular night. Their personal and business commitments could have left them somewhat unprepared, fatigued, even emotionally drained, so that they are not at their peak. Once in a competitive situation, superior athletes perform to the best of what they are capable of under any circumstances. This could be below their all-time best, but that doesn't matter. What does is that they took from within themselves what was available and used it. Unfortunately, most athletes shortchange themselves. They may have a sloppy, subpar or even terrible performance depending on their needs, conscious and unconscious feelings, and misgivings.

Psychologically weak athletes are not able to transcend the

feelings and influences that have the power to pull them down. They are not focused within themselves or clearly aware of what is happening. Most sadly, they do not realize that they are letting slip by an important moment in their lives they will never have again. This moment can lay another brick in the formation of their negative self-concept, becoming an influential factor in their future athletic underachieving.

Athletes who let the moment slip away, especially in an important competition, do so at a time when they could reap the benefits of all their hard work. Dedicated athletes structure their lives around their sport. The major part of their days revolves around training. When they practice and more particularly perform, they live out concretely the primary emphasis and meaning of their lives. Taking up practice and competition with a less than total presence is not living life to the fullest. Most athletes are not getting the most out of their time, energy, and lives.

The familial, historical and developmental issues addressed in earlier chapters now reappear. The way people train and compete tells where they have come from and what they have learned from others in their lives about sport and self-worth. Many athletes have golden opportunities both to actualize their dreams and achieve success. These golden opportunities slip through their fingers because of their psychological makeup and certain important experiences in their lives. They tense up, become apathetic or even feel the pain and emptiness of their highly specialized and often unbalanced lives right at the moment that the stakes are the highest and they are closest to picking the athletic fruit that they have cultivated their whole lives.

The gist is that people only have so much control over their lives. Skills must be developed to give athletes a fighting chance to succeed. This control is their slim hold on their destinies. The only way to enhance the chances of success is to be prepared physically and mentally for the situation that tests their mettle. Situations where one is well fed, rested and emotionally content are extremely rare. People are always, to varying degrees, overwhelmed by the demands of life, and made to perform under less-than-ideal conditions. Life calls us when it wants to and not when we are always ready, but we must respond. Athletes, especially professionals, who receive some kind of financial compensation for their performances, must perform now whether they feel like it or not.

Emotional stability has much to do with whether or not athletes will be able to exert any control over all the factors that come together in an athletic moment. Their ability to control a situation lies largely in their mental strength. This is developed and tested in the everyday routines of training. Pushing oneself on a daily basis requires tremendous mental fortitude.

Ideally, all athletes should be able to do what is required of them in the present, but this is extremely difficult when it seems like nothing is at stake, especially in practice. Routine practices are normally a grind, and it is easy to mentally relax and "blow them off." That little extra focus on form, technique, and pushing oneself through the conditioning drills pays off in the long run. No career is built in one day, one week, or one year — it typically takes years of sweat. Quality in daily workouts adds up to quality in performance and quality of one's life. Muddling through day after day will produce a muddled existence. Living life to the fullest must begin in day-to-day routines. Life is not like the movies where every moment is exciting and titillating; it is slow, commonplace, and laborious — the place where champions are forged. This awareness and attitude is not a platitude for some athletes; they live it out daily, passing through the fires of life. This attitude results from facing the truths and limits of both human and personal existence. Pete Rose, the Cincinnati Reds' manager, is a living example of an individual who lives out this kind of attitude, truly earning his nickname, "Charlie Hustle."

The ultimate challenge for all is to excel under adversity. Psychologically strong athletes rise to the occasion when things are bleakest. Some even crave adversity because it calls them to summon up strength from places that they did not know existed. There is a super high that comes from being pushed to the limit, especially on "bad days." At these times they are flirting with the edge of their personal limitations, confronting the thin line that distinguishes the great from mediocre athletes. Here athletes try to go beyond what is ordinary. Many people will seek to avoid the situation or to find an easy way out under these circumstances. For example, an athlete trying to win a 10,000-meter race when he is sick may seem crazy, but not to the superior athlete. Once he has decided to be on the track, he will not hold back. It would have been fine to decide to stay at home that day also. The point is that he is not ambivalent. Once he decides to run, he has to go for it, no matter what the reasons are that could legitimately keep him from competing (sickness, personal problems, depression, and so on).

Lynn Swann, the former Pittsburgh Steelers wide receiver, is a stellar example. I had the opportunity to go to high school with this tremendously gifted athlete. He always gave 100 percent, and was the greatest competitor the school ever had. Whenever there was a pressure situation, Swann was always *seeking* that spot in the contest. Other players, when there is only time for one last shot and their team is behind by one point, are looking for the exit. They do not want the responsibility of taking the last shot and are terrified of becoming the goat. Swann was always seeking the ball at these times. One night, when he pushed himself to the limit in a very important playoff game, he had a bad case of the flu and had told no one that he was sick. After playing his heart out he was carried off the court, wrapped up in a blanket, while the flu wracked his body. He would never say die. On the football field, the game was never decided until the last second when Swann was on the field. Time after time he ran back kickoffs and punts in the fading seconds for the touchdown, breaking tackle after tackle until he crossed the goal line. He was definitely one of a kind! His extraordinary physical gifts and an equally strong mentality combined to make him an athlete of unusual dimensions.

When Swann played, he seemed to be oblivious to what was around him. He was continually harassed in games by racists; their slurs only seemed to fuel his competitive urges. He was so confident of himself that head games only fired him up. The high school's athletic director said that "If he [the director] wanted to win the league tennis championship all we had to do was to give Lynn a tennis racquet." He was right, despite the fact that Swann had never played tennis.

The point of focusing on Swann is that having exceptional physical ability is not enough. Lynn's older brother was bigger, stronger, and more graceful, but not as successful, because of the emotional differences. After a highly successful high school career, the older Swann gradually faded into anonymity while Lynn went on to be an All-American in football and one of the best broad-jumpers in the world. This is a perfect example of brothers with exceptional (and similar) physical ability having different fates. The physical attributes were easy to see because they were visible to all, but it was their mental and emotional differences that separated them from glory in one case to anonymity in another. The issue here is not intelligence but emotional strength and stability.

Despite the fact that most athletes do not have the physical gifts of Lynn Swann, they can still develop their mental and emotional capacities. The case of the Swann brothers is a perfect example of the importance of one's mental makeup. There have been many athletes over the years with the physical skills of a Lynn Swann, but they lacked the tenacity and never-say-die attitude that come from emotional stability. Consequently, they weren't in the same league with a Lynn Swann. We will now look at how someone like Swann could so totally give himself to the moment and actually perform better as the pressure increased and in the face of adversity (sitting on the bench for two years at University of Southern California and suffering several concussions in the pros). Whatever the setbacks or obstacles were, he would always come back stronger and refused to be crushed by adversity.

To perform maximally, athletes need to be free mentally and physically. This is the primary thrust of sports psychology. Athletes must understand the full ramifications of this and at the same time get in touch with the deeper psychological structure of their overall makeup. With this awareness, athletes will be able to more fully develop their potential, and it will help them be at peace with themselves and their life circumstances. It will facilitate their chances of an unfettered and maximally efficient expression of their athletic selves.

The question still remains, Why are so many athletes crushed by the significance they attach to their perceived failures? Answering this tells why some athletes' performances are so erratic while others' are so consistent.

All athletes carry within them a storehouse of memories that have accumulated from the beginning of their lives, especially the early years at home. Their youthful interactions with parents leave an indelible impression on how they look at the world and feel about themselves. Sometimes the unconscious mind becomes the repository of very painful and distorted messages in the sense that children interpret the meaning of certain events improperly.

More typically, the parents project their "psychic garbage" on their kids. This can take many forms. Parents, because of their successes or failures, could give their children the impression that they are capable of achieving anything, and they end up with an overinflated sense of self-esteem. Or, they communicate through their words, actions, and lack of attention and affection that their children are ineffective or inadequate, and should never set high goals for themselves. Either extreme gives children a very distorted message of themselves, and will tragically cause them to spend their whole lives trying to shake these images.

All people carry pictures and messages about themselves that hold them back in life. These images spread out in such profound and subtle ways that sometimes people spend their whole lives trying to decipher the veracity of these messages (am I stupid, awkward, bad, a loser? and so on). People are oftentimes tormented by these labels. Their defense systems seal off the memory of these messages from their consciousness so that athletes rarely come to know the exact meaning and origin of them. They know of their existence indirectly, only feeling their side effects. These influences push them hither and thither, making the actualization of their goals twice as hard as necessary. They end up feeling that the best they can ever do is keep their head above water no matter how hard they try.

These unconscious messages often drive athletes toward certain goals for reasons they are not aware of or cannot admit to themselves because it would be too painful. Many boxers might acknowledge that they trained most of their lives to prove to their fathers that they were not sissies, and were made of the same stuff as they (or were not sissies like the fathers, but cut from rougher cloth). Perhaps very early a father communicated such a feeling quite strongly to his son. The message is rarely verbal. A child who must be like his macho father, may perceive himself as inadequate in this regard and feel so much shame that he refuses to be anything but macho. He then has to overcompensate to stave off the very real possibility that he may be perceived as weak at times. Such a fighter is going to be in so much emotional conflict (pulled in contrary directions) that his chances of success, despite his boxing gifts, will be greatly impaired. Being in this ambivalent and conflicting situation typically leads to feelings of burn out and depression because the stress is too great to handle. Depression is a result of being caught between two pincers; they exclude athletes' personal needs and force them to let go of who they are. Anger is often a side effect of betraying themselves. In the case of the boxer, this could be directed against his father because of his insistence on being macho and against his mother because of her Pollyannish approach to the brutality of the world, or against himself for his own inability to stand up to two domineering parents. There are countless variations on these parental themes.

Depending on the constellation of his personal dynamics with his parents, his worst or best fight could be either against gentle or macho fighters. In the ring, he may vent the rage that is meant for his father on these "tough guy" fighters, or outside it toward those "tough guy" individuals who resemble his father and ridiculed him when he was younger. Conversely, he could wilt in their terrifying presence like he did as a kid before his dad, feeling that it is pretentious to think he could beat a fighter who, in his unconscious, is an incarnation of the kind of man he perceived his father to be, and that he is not. This perception started when he was young and overpowered by his domineering father. His inferiority at that tender age was based on his father's unfair advantages — age and ability. This impression, regardless of its validity, can incapacitate a man who is in the prime of his life and is objectively no longer at a disadvantage in regard to any man in his weight class. The power of the mind can distort any objective reality.

Depression could be the result of not realizing his goals fast enough. He may find that he is working too long and hard to have the magical affirmation of manhood laid on his troubled brow. Consequently, any failures along the way may severely shake him, making him think that his father's judgment of him (of being less than a man) may be true. He may redouble his efforts like an aging ox trying to beat off the inevitability of the slaughterhouse by another extraordinary day of work.

This fighter will be lonely and emotionally needy because he didn't get X or Y from his parents. His loneliness is an inevitable by-product of his heavy training schedule and the fact that he cannot allow himself to be who he really is (perhaps a gentle, sensitive person who abhors violence). Not having the capacity to show who he is precludes the possibility of others getting close to him. He cannot risk others getting close enough to catch a glimpse of what he is most ashamed of and what he has suffered all his life from — his softness. This loneliness may be quite acute: He took up boxing specifically to obtain love and affection from certain people and not for the joy of his craft. Because of his ambivalent motives, which are unconscious, toward the sport, he will probably be further from the realization of his goals the harder he tries. Therefore, boxing for him is a means to an end, but it is not really an end in itself, because it will most likely be his demise. Competing with the primary purpose of insuring love and self esteem is a risky business, and having to succeed in order to secure these rewards is too dangerous because in many ways a sport's primary gratifications are found in other areas.

Sadly, when children get powerful negative messages, directly or indirectly, they will spend the rest of their lives trying to disprove or dispel the agonizing feelings caused by them. This, unfortunately, is hard to do. The messages burrow deeply within the folds of children's identities. A powerful effect on athletes is that they come to believe (typically subconsciously) that they are unworthy and undeserving of success. They unfortunately end up buying into these negative judgments lock, stock and barrel. Athletes constantly undermine their chances of success, and give up control of their careers, with these monsters in the basement of their identities. Oftentimes, as athletes get close to success, it becomes harder for them to succeed because of these internal conflicts. Their strongest opponent is themselves in the form of a negative self image or persona. An athlete, depending on the nature of these messages, may feel that success has either come too easily and quickly or that it is taking too long, confirming his mediocrity. Acquiring success after too much effort cannot be tolerated because he has been stamped early with the label that he is not supposed to be successful, and the extended effort supports this earlier stigma. His youthful attempts at success had only met with scorn, rejection, alienation, and ultimately failure.

In the late 1980s, women athletes are prone to sabotaging their careers right at the moment that success is within reach. They do not want to risk the rejection of those that are so important to them, and this inevitably undermines their ability to perform. Failure, then, becomes the order of the day. Unknown to themselves, they are the ones who give the prize away. They neither know why they cannot progress, nor the reasons for their failure. They will normally be very disturbed by these failures and will consciously keep telling themselves that they did everything possible to succeed, but failure was the result.

This situation occurs frequently with other women. It also happens with men because women have been conditioned to "know their place" and not be threatening to them. These fears are real; women know that many men *and* women are threatened by their success and expertise. Women have been conditioned since birth to put affiliation and belongingness before all else. This is a difficult message to shake, but thanks to the women's movement, they are beginning to get in touch with and transcend these issues. In this way, they are able to develop themselves to the maximum as people and athletes.

Some athletes feel deep down that they do not have what it takes to be winners, usually because they did not receive the necessary love and attention from their parents. They conclude that they are not special. Or, children could receive the message (indirectly) that they are supposed to be winners. The parents' expectations could have been much too high in relation to their children's actual abilities. Children internalize their parents' expectations and make them their own, and drive themselves with strained tenacity to live up to their expectations. This is a no-win situation, because children might not have the proper motivation or natural gifts to reach the standard and goals set by their parents. Depression and guilt result when athletes realize that they are not achieving what they believe they should be. Both of these emotions affect their performance. Not attaining goals leads to guilt over failing to meet the expectations of others and themselves, creating a vicious circle: Guilt leads to poor performance, thus moving athletes further away from their goals, causing more guilt to occur. This is very common in baseball. Hitters are notorious for getting down on themselves or for getting into a slump.

The reasons are typically mental for a slump, with the exception of those caused by injury. Some crisis has occurred and the athlete is unable to weather the shock waves from it. The incident might not seem traumatic to outside observers, but it is trouble-some to the athlete. Common problems that athletes, like all peo-ple, find disturbing are related to financial issues, family trouble, unstable love relationships, poor past performances, or problems with one's status in an organization. All of these can make an ath-lete mentally off balance, depending on the severity of the cir-cumstances. These, however, are not the subtle psychological issues that typically topple careers. Those may appear as super-ficial to the outside observer, but they take root in a much more secluded part of the experiencer's psyche.

As mentioned earlier, life's crises are taken in stride by ath-letes who have a stable identity. They do not have to struggle with or debate over feelings of self-worth, allowing them to focus their energy on their sport instead of repressed emotional conflicts. They do not have to deal constantly with feelings of inadequacy, whether or not they can succeed, or most importantly, deserve re-spect and success. They know, on some level, that they matter to someone, are basically likeable, and that people are drawn to them. Athletes without this sense of security are emotionally fra-gile, temperamental, unstable and skittish. Life crises and personal setbacks affect them much more profoundly, because their main objective is to bolster a feeble identity through athletic prowess. Anything that threatens their sense of wholeness or security will prove to undermine their athletic gifts, ability to perform, and per-sonal life. Emotionally stable athletes can deal with life's problems more easily. They can keep things in perspective. Their game is less affected by the uncertainty of life and the sports world in particular because their identities are not totally invested in athletic ac-complishment. They know there is much more to life than just sports, and they do not need sports to justify their lives and self-worth.

Many things can break an athlete's spirit, whether it is lack of playing time, a vote of no confidence from a coach, or an injury. Some survive and others are irreparably damaged. Some carry on out of the sheer terror of having nothing else to fall back on for money, status, and self-worth. They are fighting for their emo-tional lives, either trying to confirm or disconfirm others' judg-ments and expectations. Some are hooked on the limelight and public acclaim; for them, to be average is to be nobody. There is an entire subculture that supports this view. The addiction to be special or a star — as heady as it is — often has its roots in those who are alienated from people. Acclaim becomes a substitute for intimacy and affection. People in this category do not know how to exist in a relationship of equality and reciprocity with another human being; athletic achievement is the only way they know how to draw people toward them.

Athletes are human beings, are confronted with the harshness and difficulties of life, and need a stable, emotional and personal life just as anyone else does. An added complication is that athletes are under tremendous pressure because in competition they are constantly scrutinized and evaluated. They can never rest on their laurels because it is a struggle to stay on top. Keeping afloat emotionally in life demands the majority of people's energy, attention, and resources. Trying to go beyond the day-to-day demands (food, money, stable environment) to excel and transcend the commonplace involves much emotional and financial support, natural talent, courage, and determination. If the foundation of an athlete's personality is weak, he will never build a high rise. The athletic world is a microcosm of a story that is lived out in all walks of life. Athletes who achieve world-class status are the crème de la crème. They are the ones who have been able to go beyond the ordinary to deal with all of life's demands and still develop something beyond the basic needs of survival. They have gone beyond just "making it" to creating something, and have actualized goals within a doubly competitive lifestyle.

Many athletes of world-class caliber get scorched the closer they get to the limelight of stardom. Pressure, competition and rewards increase as they go higher. To make the trip, all athletes must keep developing themselves physically and emotionally to meet the growing requirements demanded by excellence. Many who cannot keep up turn to artificial means to keep afloat. Cocaine is the panacea of many who find themselves overwhelmed and depleted by the pressures of top-flight competition. Drug addiction is a common affliction of many professional athletes today. Cocaine, especially, seems to be the ideal drug for those whose sport depends on high levels of energy and self-confidence.

Life in professional basketball can be a grind: Three games a week in three different cities, a fast-paced game with a twenty-four second clock, and the run and gun style of play the rule. This can be devastatingly brutal. Very few have that kind of stamina. The financial rewards are so great that athletes are destroying their minds, bodies, and personal lives to grab their piece of the professional pie. To bolster their fading chances, they often turn to the seemingly miraculous powers of this white powder, an elixir that gives them fuel to burn and feelings of confidence to make up for their ever-increasing personal inadequacies and insecurities. Cocaine temporarily covers the holes in athletes' personal makeup that they have to work through, compensate for, or acknowledge throughout different phases of their adult lives.

Optimal performance is no easy feat. It involves a whole complex of personal and interpersonal factors. Its cornerstone lies in people's ability to be focused and centered with a clear understanding of who they are and what a situation means to them. For some highly gifted athletes, optimal performance is more natural or instinctive than it is for others. Most athletes must make a conscious effort to ground themselves in the importance of the situation that they now find themselves in. The ability comes with maturity, a sharp comprehension of what they are actually doing. This usually comes from "having been there" many times before. Mature athletes have typically failed under pressure more than a few times. They learned from their mistakes, especially that of putting too much of their identity fulfillment both in the hands of others and in their athletic accomplishments. Once athletes get beyond this attitude, they are halfway toward success. They become their own person and develop a much finer appreciation of the absurdity and irrationality of those who structure and control the world of their athletic pursuits.

Optimal performance is being one with your situation and not being taken off center by a multitude of internal and external distractions. It involves the letting go of one's fears and expectations; it means a willingness to let the situation happen but to strive to control how it should happen.

10

How to Get Attuned
to Your Athletic Self

This chapter is a summation. It provides an easy way for all athletes to begin to know those dimensions of their personalities that come together in a unique way to form their athletic selves, enabling them to recognize their strengths and liabilities. This knowledge puts athletes in a more advantageous position in regard to their aspirations. There are several ways for them to look at certain aspects of their athletic lives to find out what is either blocking or facilitating their pursuits. Athletes will be aided by analyzing their style, the way they train and compete, and handle stress, injury and failure. The themes emerging from analysis of one's style will help form a picture of psychological strength and weakness (including an awareness of one's emotional stability, true motivation, and capabilities) and their historical roots. Once athletes find the contentment that results from such knowledge, they will be able to move closer to excellence. Everyone should be able to increase the quality of his performances and personal enjoyment over the long haul by a good measure as a result of coming to know himself.

There are six dimensions of athletics that I wish to take up in this book. Knowledge of all six can help all athletes become attuned to their constitutions.

Reacting to Coaches

All athletes run into people with whom they cannot get along. Certain players, coaches, managers, or teachers seem to rub them the wrong way. Some athletes cannot produce for coaches who are the strict, authoritarian, hard-nosed, Vince Lombardi type. They rebel, become lethargic or tense, upset, even terrified and commonly, passive-aggressive when working with such a coach, doing as little as possible of what the coach demands. They go through the motions but are not really emotionally committed to what they are doing. In reality, even though these players may be holding onto their positions or could be getting back at the coach for the way they are being treated, they end up hurting only their own careers. These coaches may be perceived as uncaring, overly demanding and insensitive to personal differences, resulting in athletes' resentment of being put into an impersonal mold and treated as unimportant.

It is possible for some athletes to be treated insensitively their whole lives, whether by parents, siblings, other relatives, teachers, or coaches, with few resources to fight back. Subconsciously or consciously, they may never forget the pain and feelings of humiliation at these earlier times. Feeling that their identities were being wrested from them, they may become determined never to let this happen again. As a result, certain athletes, upon encountering overbearing coaches, could find their careers foreshortened. The athletes are typically unaware of the deep-rooted nature of their personal resentment towards the coach. These athletes are saying through their actions that they cannot be motivated or forced to perform well when treated in this manner. The athlete is getting emotional equilibrium by hurting another and failing to realize whom he or she is hurting most. Athletes fail in order to get what little ego integrity they have together and to make the coach (or "substitute parent") feel embarrassed or powerless. All parties involved, not forgetting the fans, are the losers.

At the opposite extreme, there are some players who perform at their highest levels for this kind of coach. Bobby Knight, coach of the 1984 United States Men's Olympic Basketball Team, seems to fit this image. Some players, because of the constitution of their personalities, are more dependent than others. They need someone they respect and are afraid of. Such a coach gets their competitive juices flowing. These athletes are more accustomed to being told what to do, and are afraid to incur his wrath if they do not follow his orders. They could possibly fear personal rejection and condemnation if they do not perform up to the level of the coach's expectations. For whatever reasons—dependency, passivity, lethargy, terror, or lack of personal motivation—these athletes get going when the whip is on their backs. Obviously, those fitting into this category are deeply influenced by forceful personalities. In their personal lives, their greatest trauma or crisis may have been failing to please those who had power over them, most likely their parents. The child may have been shamed or ridiculed for his or her failures, and does not desire to experience this feeling again. Athletes fitting this description are literally driving themselves in order to avoid the wrath and rejection of those in charge. They cannot relax because on some level they are trying to protect themselves psychologically.

Others perform at their best with a hard-driving, domineering coach because their personal hatred of the coach fuels them on. Their project is to excel, which creates a protective space for themselves in which the coach cannot hurt them. They feel that their level of performance insures them against criticism and being dominated. They have learned early in life that actions speak louder than words. If they can perform well, they will be left alone and show those who threaten or drive them down that they are superior. They transcend and silence those in authority who are trying to eradicate their originality and style. The message is that if they perform well, they will not be harassed, and will be left alone to handle their lives and sport in their own way.

All these athletes are quite vulnerable; they are attempting to excel for less than the best of reasons. They are trying to protect their sense of identity in reaction to certain powerful individuals, and have not grown enough emotionally to be able to get beyond specific psychological fears and insecurities. Growth in these weak areas can only help them to be better in their approach to sports in general, and specifically with their actual performances. Mature and centered athletes do not define their lives and careers in terms of threats, judgments, standards, and expectations of others. If one can move out of this defensive posture, one will be much less vulnerable to frustration, feelings of incompetence, and failure to realize potential. Athletes who can recognize who they work best with can learn much about their own psychological makeup. This enables them to seek out coaches with styles that complement the athletes' psychological strengths and weaknesses. When athletes are aware of their qualities from knowing the kinds of coaches they work best with, they become more emotionally aware and secure, thus less vulnerable to the whims of coaches who could ruin them.

Some perform best with low-key and sensitive coaches. Carl Lewis, the great track and field athlete, is an example. Many rigid and insecure coaches gave no promise for Lewis' career or talents. Several believed he was uncoachable, since he would not follow their coaching regimens. Lewis was too independent. He would not do something he did not believe was right for him. In college, he met a coach, Tellez, who was secure enough to offer coaching advice to him. Lewis has since gone on to win numerous meets with record-setting performances.

Independent athletes feel unthreatened, appreciated, and at ease with respectful coaches, and have a sense of enough personal space to be themselves. If they have never experienced this respect before, the difference can be striking. Such players drop their defensiveness and truly blossom. All athletes know that they play their best for a coach who appreciates their ability. At these times, their confidence level rises and they play relaxed with self-assuredness. This is the ideal space to be in.

Strange things can happen in this atmosphere, however. Dependent athletes may not respond well to this second kind of coach—they may relax and become unmotivated. The dependent nature of their personalities prevents them from being able to push themselves without the presence of a "whip master." They eventually realize that their motives for competing and training are out of fear of loss (dignity, esteem, and love) rather than the love of the game or more mature personal motives. Without the intimidation and the motivating energy of an authoritative coach, they are confronted with their personal inadequacies and insubstantial motivations. They cannot adjust to having latitude and personal responsibility to train on their own without any pressure from the coach. These people are not used to performing in a less structured competitive environment, and feel lost in a personal sea composed of motivations that are not founded in personal freedom and choice. A real possibility is that they eventually get disoriented and lost without an authoritarian coach with a firm presence. With very little sense of personal motivation and a lack of coping skills (the ability to handle trying situations on their own), their careers flounder or end abruptly.

At the opposite extreme, these athletes could begin to grow as independent people. The pressure of being thrown back on themselves may catapult them into confronting their limitations and their reasons for being in the sport. If so, a new and potent dimension of their personalities and careers could develop.

There are some who are primarily dependent on others for their motivation to train and compete, but in a different way from those just described. These athletes thrive on competition with coaches, players, and power dynamics in general. They have to discover new sources of motivation when exposed to a less authoritarian coach, for they are really into drama. The fuel of their lives is generated by getting into problems or personality conflicts with those in power. As long as these athletes have someone to push against, they feel important and therefore secure. They know who they are by drawing the lines of demarcation clearly between themselves and those attempting to direct them.

This is very similar to the way adolescents structure their relationships to their parents (they resent their parents' authority and rebel against it, but are simultaneously lost without it). Being on their own without any structure at this time in their lives is terrifying; they only feel strong in relation to someone else who is strong. Within this clearly defined power dynamic they can fully express their talents, and feel safe within clearly defined limits. Without these limits, they are confused as to how to proceed and set limits for themselves. Also, they are thrown back on the questions of who they are and what they want in this particular phase of their lives, specifically the competitive environment. Power conflicts are used as a means to answer these questions. In this way, athletes can decide to avoid standing alone without someone to blame or fight with. Standing alone is difficult for them, because then they have to take responsibility for their actions and the course of their lives.

On the other hand, if they fail as anonymous teammates they are not alone. When standing alone others can rejoice at their failures, at their audacity for trying to follow their own star when the masses huddle together out of their dread of uniqueness. When athletes fail within an organizational framework (the coaches', not their own) they do not have to take all the blame. When the independent ones fail they soon come to realize that most people are merciless. Through their failures, independent athletes warn everyone not to take chances. Most people smile inwardly when the "high flyers" are shot down, returned to anonymity and forced to seek security like the rest of the team. Athletes who consciously plan their future, irrespective of potential conflict and unconcerned with the power dynamics with those in authority, tread a perilous but nevertheless potentially fruitful and exhilarating path.

Athletes must become aware of the personality profiles of those coaches, administrators, and competitors who affect them in a manner that facilitates their careers. Those who know well their temperament will choose to work with coaches they are most compatible with. In learning the characteristics of their personalities and the context within which they operate best, people will ideally put themselves in an environment where there are people they work best with. They can begin to discover what it is about certain individuals that affects them positively or negatively, and what it is about themselves that causes them to respond better to some people than to others. Athletes can then get in touch with their weak points and the modes of interaction they use when confronting those who have power over them. Most importantly, they can discover that certain ways of reacting to authority may have been appropriate at an earlier and more vulnerable age, but now the responses, being possibly neurotic and problematic are limited, even destructive to their careers and feelings of self-worth.

Athletes who are passive-aggressive in the face of overbearing coaches are living out a technique they learned very early in life. This reaction is reasonable for children because it allows them to resist without clearly acknowledging that they are actually doing so. They can also avoid punishment. Being passive-aggressive does not just mean refusing commands; it can be a slow response or a performance so incompetent that it might as well have been a refusal. For adults, this stance leads to confrontation and most likely a deterioration of an already submissive situation. Being passive-aggressive gives the illusion of compliance, and it is very hard to pin these people down. They both do and not do what is requested at the same time.

Again, passive-aggressive behavior may have been a semiappropriate way of expressing anger and disagreement on the part of children. It is understandable that youths try to communicate their feelings of being dominated in this indirect manner. They are not in a position of equality with those who have all the power in the relationship, and lack the physical, mental, and other resources to communicate their feelings directly. It is an unequal and unjust relationship.

As athletes mature, these inequalities even out and they should begin to develop new and more appropriate ways of interacting with authority figures. Athletes should realize, as they mature, that they have more fire power than they did when they were children. Additionally, their current coaches may be more just than their parents or former teachers and coaches were. Consequently, young athletes should realize that they have more options in dealing with and reacting to the dictates of an authoritarian coach. They are now — or should be — more knowledgeable and imaginative about the various ways of relating to coaches.

Reacting to Competitors

There are certain kinds of opponents that commonly throw people off balance or get them psyched out. All athletes need to know why they can perform better against some competitors than they can against others.

Competing against those one likes, dislikes, or doesn't know all address something different in athletes. Some perform best against their friends, having gotten a strong message when they were young that they were safe with those they felt closest to. They would not be rejected or hurt for competing in this intimate environment, and feel that *healthy* competition exists.

Some on the other hand, subconsciously subvert their chances of winning against people that they like or are friendly with. This is especially true of women who have been conditioned to put affiliation and group needs before their own. Others have poor performances so as not to make waves — they either feel guilty for beating their friends, fear exclusion or rejection from the group, or feel within themselves that their victories make them appear pretentious. This could have its roots in earlier childhood experiences, when as a result of threatening others with a superior performance, they received the cold shoulder as a response. Many learn that success threatens and alienates people.

Conversely, athletes may do poorly against others they know well because they are aware of their opponents' personal problems and tribulations. This is especially true in regard to teammates. If one athlete cares for another, he may feel guilty for beating him, especially if the opponent is losing confidence because of several subpar performances or personal difficulties. Bill Russell, while at the University of San Francisco, permitted his friend Johnny Mathias to beat him out for a position on the 1956 Olympic track team, as a high jumper. Russell knew he had a pro career to look forward to and Mathias' future seemed less promising at that time. In other situations, one athlete might know that his opponent worked harder and struggled longer than he, and therefore is more deserving of victory.

In view of this, many athletes do not want to get too close to their opponents. The closer they get, the more they get to know their opponents as real people, and become sympathetically affected by their personal needs. This explains why boxers often have to work up a feeling of hatred for their opponents in order to achieve the necessary level of brutality that the sport demands.

Many athletes are caring individuals, knowing the pain and needs of others. They may come to realize that winning does not mean as much to them as to their opponents, so they (usually subconsciously) hold themselves back in competition. The ethic of putting others' needs before your own takes hold. Those who believe this could even feel that it is wrong to want to claim their own birthright in sports based on their natural talent and hard work. They may feel, subconsciously, that it is morally wrong to aspire to the exclusive and pretentious position of a champion, especially when one has to crush opponents on the road to the top.

At the other end of the spectrum, some athletes perform best against those they dislike. Sport is a socially acceptable arena in which to express aggression and anger. Competitive athletics for many provides a perfect environment to dominate those that one does not like. Some athletes can pull out all the "stops" against disliked opponents. They are not concerned with their opponents' needs and feelings, wanting instead to crush them. Sports are used as a weapon to subdue or conquer those whom one dislikes.

Others feel ashamed at wanting to destroy the opponents they dislike. Their upbringing schooled them to believe that they should be compassionate and not develop aggressive rivalries. They hold back against opponents that they have a personal distaste for, because guilt feelings about openly disliking and wanting to destroy someone are deeply rooted in their subconscious. Many times, these feelings are traceable all the way back to childhood, when parents and teachers forcefully preached the dictates of compassion, forgiveness and tolerance, especially toward those who have wronged one. Consciously, the athlete may want to dominate or destroy a disliked opponent, but the subconscious messages of his or her youth get the upper hand, installing a more pacific attitude. This kind of internal conflict usually undermines an athlete's confidence, concentration and presence to the task at hand.

Still others feel most at ease with a competitor they do not know well. They do not have to worry about personal feelings of guilt, success, or crushing their opponents' egos and dreams. They may never see them again. Since they do not know their opponents, they have nothing to worry about. They are concerned with neither what the other athlete is going through emotionally nor what his or her talents are.

Another variation is that some athletes not weighted down by competitive urges and aggression are not motivated against unknown opponents because they have nothing to base a grudge on. They need some kind of personal conflict in order to get pumped up. Without interpersonal tension, they are pushed back on themselves to discover a different motivation that will provide enough impetus for them to be successful. These same athletes may even get psyched out by not knowing anything about their competitors. Unknown factors tend to weigh on them, and their minds run wild, creating all sorts of possibilities and imagined calamities. This increases their anxiety levels to the point of choking.

All these athletes just described have deep-rooted feelings stirred up when they face certain opponents. They must get in touch with the personal characteristics of those athletes that they either can or cannot perform well against, and discover what buttons (vulnerable spots) get pushed when they face different athletes. They can then begin to discover, work through, and ultimately comprehend when these pushbuttons originated and how they continue to be maintained. For example, a person is psyched out and backs down from a cocky, belligerent and seemingly tough opponent: What can he gain from this? First, he would not have to face himself and his limits if he gave it his best and still lost. Secondly, he can keep his current sense of self intact because winning might mean having to become aggressive and animal-like, something he does not want to be. These are exactly the qualities that he despises in his opponents and in others, and his deepest sensibilities are offended by them. Not wanting to become like them, he subconsciously understands that if he has to be that way, then he does not want to win and may even want out of the sport.

This is a very difficult judgment for an athlete to accept, especially one who has devoted a large portion of his or her life to the sport and is highly invested in what it does for ego and financial status. Such invested satisfaction gives athletes many reasons to not become aware of what these opponents represent to them. On a deeper level they could have similarly aggressive, cocky, and domineering feelings, yet the structure of their identities and the nature of their interpersonal relationships will not tolerate such feelings and their accompanying actions. Athletes will probably repress the feelings and respond with disgust and unconscious envy to those who are able to live them out freely. In order to protect who they are (and shouldn't be) they back down in the presence of cocky opponents and let them dominate.

Athletes, therefore, gain a great deal by not allowing these psychological sensitive spots or buttons to be pushed, even if it means defeating themselves. Consequently, they maintain a sense of self that they can live with and in which they obviously have a large investment. The problem is that in certain situations this runs counter to their athletic aspirations. Sense of self is preserved but the cost of victory is high; their capacity for achievement is impaired and their longed-for athletic dreams seriously jeopardized.

Catcalls and Razzing

As mentioned earlier, all athletes are susceptible to head games. They must be clear in their own minds what kinds of head games affect them negatively, and which ones fire them up to the point of maximum efficiency.

Some athletes get very disturbed by razzing or being the butt of jokes or ridicule. Obviously, public ridicule is a serious source of pain and embarrassment. These athletes are being touched in a vulnerable part of their personalities. Their confidence may be shaken by taunts because they are unsure of their capabilities and preparations to begin with. Those who are in sport to prove something (that they are not losers, or that they are "real men" or "real women") are most sensitive to razzing. Those not having to prove these things and without the psychic scars associated with them are far less vulnerable to razzing and will typically ignore it. Depending on the personal makeup of an athlete's identity she or he will be extremely sensitive to certain issues and not to others. No two athletes will respond identically to the same type of razzing.

Other athletes' performances are greatly affected by knowing that they are not liked or highly regarded by their opponents. It hurts them not to be with the "in group," and to experience the boos, jeers and ridicule. Every athlete is influenced by these kinds of reactions, some more than others. Athletes with stable personal lives are less swayed by the feelings and actions of their competitors, teammates and the general public. Others could be in the game largely for public acclaim and approval; not to receive it hurts them deeply.

Razzing is something that all athletes have dealt with at one time or another. They need to know what gets to them (hearing that they are no good, a loser, ugly, too fat or skinny or too weak, or slurs about race, religion and family). Athletes may feel insecure about any one or all these characteristics, a very human reaction. All people have flaws *and* have failed to receive certain emotional nutrients during their personal evolution. Last, since we live in a racist, fadist culture, athletes will always be fair game for any individual waiting to take a potshot at them. Until they become consciously aware of what these characteristics mean and why they are so sensitive to these issues they will often be at the mercy of the fickle public. Inability to handle these personal slurs dooms their chances of success.

The Meaning of Failure

Athletes need to know what kinds of athletic and personal setbacks deeply and negatively affect them. Some are crushed by losses, injuries, illnesses, being benched, feeling unappreciated, or the end of a romantic relationship. Losses force all athletes to reevaluate what they have been doing that has contributed to the losses. As long as failures are not too frequent and are interspersed with successes, athletes can begin to see through their failures and discover their shortcomings.

Some competitors are floored by failure and find it intolerable. It shakes them to the core, and they project a failure in one situation to their whole lives. They feel worthless, inadequate, and unimportant. These are the athletes described in Chapter 1. They bought the message, most typically from their parents, that their self-worth is directly proportional to their success and performance. In order not to be crushed athletically and personally, they need to realize what is driving and terrorizing them subconsciously in relation to the possibility of failure. They need to become aware of why sport is a "life or death" affair for them. They are trying to keep their identities afloat with the main goal of not having others discover that they are merely ordinary, subject to failure, and therefore unworthy of love and respect. They also need to realize that their self-worth is *not* reducible to achievement quotas; such a message is nonsense. It is distortive and unloving, and can stunt their personal growth and happiness. They need to feel the rage that they have suppressed for years in regard to these manipulative messages and discover what it is within themselves that is valuable and worthy of appreciation. If they fail to do this, their lives will be anxious, driven, and unhappy, and they will be constantly buffeted by the whims of fate and the sports public.

Some get very upset by injuries and illnesses, feeling at these times that the rug has been pulled out from under them. Illnesses and injuries test the fortitude of every athlete, but some can come back with renewed determination, sometimes reaching even greater heights. Bart Conners, the gymnast, is a case in point. He suffered an extremely debilitating injury to his elbow and shoulder. After several operations and a herculean rehabilitation program, he came back in one short year to win a gold medal in the 1984 Summer Olympics. His efforts during the games exceeded any performance that he had accomplished prior to them.

There are other athletes who never completely recover physically or emotionally from an injury or illness. Many, because of their upbringing, culture, and personal talents, always had it pretty easy. They neither knew struggle or severe adversity, nor did they ever have to put their nose to the grindstone. They lived in a protected environment and never had to face the cruel realities of life (that they are vulnerable, mortal and not ultimately in control of their lives and bodies). For them, an unexpected dose of reality can be devastating. They might not have the skills, stamina, self-confidence or motivation to push on in the face of adversity. More typically, their reasons for pursuing a sport are not self-generated. Athletes driving themselves to reach some imagined goal that will once and for all salvage their shaky identities are quite vulnerable to being devastated by an injury or a perceived failure. They do not have the right attitude to handle setbacks. An injury signifies to them that they are getting further away from their desperately needed achievements. Those, however, who are in the sport for personal reasons (with a commitment beyond its day-to-day fulfillments) will weather the storms and go on. Time and certain achievements are not their primary motivators; self improvement and the love of the sport propel them.

Athletes must confront their true motivation for competing when they face the stark realities of human existence. After failure they must dig deeply into their motivational bag to discover why they are doing this. What reasons do they have to come back from a serious injury, illness, or defeat? This is where the athlete's mettle proves out. Self-confidence, motivation and the ability to cope with suffering are severely tested when people find themselves caught up in adversity.

Being benched or feeling unappreciated by coaches, team-mates, and loved ones can hit athletes as hard as injuries. They must become attuned to whatever it is they are doing that does not meet the demands or the expectations of those who hold the strings over their careers and feelings of self-worth. Who holds the strings is important. Being benched or unappreciated may not mean that athletes will not play on this or any other team, or that they may not be appreciated in another environment and by different in-dividuals. It is in respect to the current individuals that the athlete is having difficulty. This must be understood because it puts the problem in context and does not make the athlete dependent on the judgment of certain people. Athletes must question why they are not meeting the particular standards of these people. Are the stan-dards contrary to their personal goals, talents, and style? Likewise, do they resist dictates because of certain insecurities or fears and an inability to adapt and let others have influence over them?

These athletes might be in an environment that is inhospitable to the personal issues they are struggling with. They should begin to ask why it is so difficult for them to make the necessary ad-justments to the demands of an athletic context (team or official, for instance). Or, the athlete can begin to search for a more com-patible coach, team, institution, or organization if he or she feels that compromise would result in a loss of self, the spark and direc-tion that are uniquely his or her own.

Training

Another way to find out how one is psychologically connected to one's sport is to reflect on how relaxed one is during practice, and how much enjoyment one gets out of training. This also holds for important contests. Are athletes obsessed with their sport? Can they sleep, eat and be generally relaxed during training and com-petition and in their free time? The answer to that will determine how much of their identities and self-esteem is invested in their athletic pursuits.

Most athletes are fairly relaxed in their practice routines, and only occasionally, tense, upset, or ill at ease. Normally, if there is some stress in their lives, it is probably because of some new aspect of training being introduced, or an abrupt change in practice routines. Occasionally, driven athletes are uptight during workouts. They feel that they must get every ounce of benefit possible out of their training. Such obsessions are rewarded in some cases, but typically, lead to burn out and depression. Athletes who punish themselves sometimes get to the top; others subjected to that kind of self-inflicted pressure usually snap like a too-tightly wound guitar string. The self punishers may feel that unless they are always pushing themselves, they will eventually either fall behind their competitors, fail to get what they want, or fail altogether. Obviously, they have an extremely high investment in their ability to achieve athletically. Much of their self-worth is rooted not only in their success, but also in preventing themselves from ending up in a position of failure.

Similarly, many get very anxious before an important competition. This is fairly common, because such events signify that their sense of self is going to be evaluated, possibly challenged, or even strongly threatened. A failure in an important competition will have profound effects on their sense of self. The closer they get temporally to this event, the closer they get to discovering whether they are who they think they are (a winner, a champion, a loser, a choker, or just plain mediocre). They will either live up to their personal expectations or they will fail. Either way, they will see themselves differently depending on the outcome of the event. For them, there is no middle ground, only success or failure. With so much riding on the event, it is understandable why some athletes get so tense even days before it. They are looking to bolster their shaky ego with a concrete achievement. Such athletes define who they are by what they do in relation to tangible accomplishments. This is both normal and somewhat neurotic, the latter because no one can ever totally define himself by external achievement. Every person is so much more and less than any one particular achievement.

Many athletes have their whole physiological and psychological system thrown out of whack a short time before an important event. They become hypersensitive and grouchy, and their sleeping and eating habits are disturbed. They are very vulnerable during these times. The degree and severity of this anxiety will tell an athlete a great deal about who he or she should and shouldn't become. Is the athlete willing to listen to the messages of anxiety?

Practically anyone in sports fears becoming the very kind of person that would otherwise be unacceptable to him or her (a failure, a loser, one who has no guts, a "chicken," an average person, or a nobody). The less an athlete is able to shake the thought of the upcoming event, the more significant it is to his or her sense of identity. This is a clear indicator of what is at stake for athletes in terms of their self-understanding, which will be redefined by the results of the upcoming athletic contest.

The importance of being clearly aware of what a particular event means to one's sense of self-esteem cannot be downplayed. Athletes who are not consciously aware of what is going on in respect to the competition are vulnerable to the disruptive events of anxiety and tension. The probability of choking or of performing in an anxious and therefore guarded manner is increased tremendously. Repressing the range of operative meanings surrounding this event opens athletes to devastation if they fail or perform below their ability. The probability of subpar performances increases when subconscious conflicts and fears rule the athlete from within. Giving up the locus of control to his or her subconscious practically guarantees a subpar performance. Hence, whatever the athlete fears the most has the best chance of happening.

The athlete who is self-possessed and listens to his emotions has a tremendous advantage over his psychologically immature and ignorant opponent. A psychologically aware athlete will hang in there and handle stress much better and longer than his more repressed competitor.

Environment and Performance

Athletes should reflect upon and question those times in their careers when everything was either going great or poorly. They should become clearly aware of what is going on in their personal and athletic lives to see how their emotional status is affecting performance. In this way, they can strive to maintain a personal environment that is most fulfilling, consistent, and stable. This will aid them in training and actual performances. There are many peripheral issues vital to athletes' sense of well-being that enable them to devote themselves more completely to their athletic tasks. The right place to live, a good love life, the emotional support of one's family, good friends, compatible coaches and teammates, and financial security are dimensions of life that, if stable and secure, can put athletes at ease and let them concentrate on athletic tasks. Informed people know that these dimensions are typically the motives for athletes' pushing themselves to succeed in the first place. Those who have all of these things already may be hard pressed to find the motivation to push themselves towards excellence. But, if they have too little in regard to these important life dimensions, they will suffer, constantly struggling to survive emotionally and psychologically. There will be little energy or impetus left for athletic endeavors.

Athletes must become aware how the various dimensions of their lives come together in the most optimal manner. They will then be able to notice when they are performing at either their best or worst. For example, some are able to concentrate or train best when they have a love relationship in which the partner is supportive and does not interfere with their pursuits. With a partner like this, they feel grounded, loved, appreciated and therefore more sure of themselves. Their confidence level is up. Having a supportive mate will make up for many emotional lacks that athletes encounter in their home lives and athletic careers.

Others are at their best when they just date or are unattached. This way, they do not feel pressured or distracted, and do not have to worry about anyone else except themselves and their athletic careers. Hence, they are at peace and centered. These athletes may have come from homes where most of their emotional needs were met. Therefore, during this phase of their lives, they are able to forgo intimate relationships, and are relatively free of neurotic demands that would require that a mate be available for their emotional support during a time when they really must struggle on their own and discipline themselves athletically.

There is another variation of those who do not want a steady mate while competing. If as children they had an intrusive mother or father, they could be reluctant to have anyone close to them while striving for excellence. Their fear is that the mate will meddle or interfere in their quest.

Every dimension of athletes' lives should be closely inspected.

Ultimately, they will then be able to allocate the proper amount of time, energy, and attention to each of the important dimensions of their lives. They will be in harmony with themselves and be able to give themselves totally to their sport. Perhaps, for the first time in their lives, they will not be competing against the unacceptable parts of their psyches, but against their actual opponents.

When athletes have worked through the questions and issues of this chapter, they should have a much clearer comprehension of those dimensions of their personality which most intensely influence their whole approach (motivation, commitment, and fears) to athletics. Knowing the ramifications of each should give them a decided advantage over their psychologically naive or ignorant opponents.

The more athletes become attuned to the repressed or unacceptable parts of their personalities, the sooner they can begin to make the necessary changes in their regimens. Accordingly, it will be much more difficult for others to push their defensive or protective "buttons." Being in tune with who they are and why they compete not only makes athletes more precise in terms of getting greater returns on their expenditure of energy, but also makes for a much more focused, intense, and therefore formidable competitor. Athletes who are in tune have few psychic gaps through which their mental strength and vitality can be dissipated, and thus used against them by others or, more ironically, by themselves.

Selected Bibliography

Alapack, Richard. *The Phenomenology of the Natural Athlete*. Ph.D. dissertation, Duquesne University, 1977.
Excellent description and analysis of the emotional and mental constitution of the natural athlete.

Asken, M. and Goodling, M. "Sports Psychology I: An Introduction and Overview." *Sports and Spokes,* June 1986, pp. 12–15.

Bleier, Rocky and O'Neil, Terry. *Fighting Back*. New York: Stein & Day, 1975.
Excellent autobiography of an athlete driven by the fear of meaningless anonymity.

Bunker, Linda, and Rotella, Robert. *Sport Psychology: Maximizing Sport Performance*. Ithaca, N.Y.: Movement Publications, 1981.

Carron, Albert. *Social Psychology of Sport: An Experimental Approach*. Ithaca, N.Y.: Movement Publications, 1981.

Cox, Richard. *Sports Psychology Concepts*. Dubuque, Iowa: William Brown Publishers, 1985.
This is a very technical introductory text to sports psychology.

It is comprehensive but too mechanistic; covers most of the major areas, but treats the athlete as a machine rather than a person.

Cratty, Bryant. *Psychology in Contemporary Sport: A Guideline for Coaches and Athletes.* Englewood Cliffs, N.J.: Prentice Hall, 1983.
This is a very good book. It is quite sensitive to the important issues in sports psychology but in a rather technical and scientific fashion.

_____. *Psychology, Preparation and Athletic Excellence.* Ithaca, N.Y.: Movement Publications, 1984.

Creekmore, C.R. "Games Athletes Play." *Psychology Today,* July 1984, pp. 40–44.

Davis, James Allen. *An Unfair Advantage: The Mental Part of Sports and Business.* Traditional Publishing, 1964.

Edwards, Harry. *Revolt of the Black Athlete.* New York: Free Press, 1969.
A pioneer work and still the best available on the exploitation of the black athlete. Clearly demonstrates the multitude of sociological, psychological and economic pressures black athletes must confront.

Fahey, Thomas. *Getting into Olympic Form.* New York: Butterick, 1980.
Specializes on the internal motivators of superior vs. mediocre athletes. Good work.

Fuller, Peter. *The Champions.* New York: Urizen Books, 1977.
This is an excellent introduction to the depth psychology components of sports. It provides a psychoanalytic understanding of the driven athlete, i.e., one who is obsessed by his or her sport.

Gallway, James. *Inner Tennis: Playing the Game.* New York: Random House, 1976.
A very good descriptive account of the nonphysical, or mental dimensions of tennis. Excellent, easy to read introduction.

Gill, Diane. *Psychological Dynamics of Sport.* Champaign, Ill.: Human Kinetics, 1986.

Harris, Betty, and Harris, Dorothy. *Athletes' Guide to Sports Psychology*. Champaign, Ill.: Human Kinetics, 1984.

Hatfield, Bradley. "Understanding Anxiety: Implications for Sports Performance." *NSCA Journal,* Volume 9, 1987.

Huizinga, Johan. *Homo Ludens.* Boston: Beacon Press, 1950.
    An old book that is still timely. For the philosophically minded, it studies man the creature who not only plays but who discovers creativity and renewal in it. A classic.

Kiester, Edwin. "The Playing Fields of the Mind." *Psychology Today,* July 1984, pp. 18–24.

Klienman, Seymour. *Mind and Body*. Champaign, Ill.: Human Kinetics, 1986.

_____. "The Nature of a Self in Its Relation to an Other in Sport." *Journal of the Philosophy of Sport,* vol. 2 (Sept. 1975), pp. 45–50.

Knauss, David R. *Peak Performance*. Englewood Cliffs, N.J.: Prentice Hall, 1980.
    A good analysis of all the negative mindsets that athletes get into that undermine their best chances of success and the actualization of their athlete gifts.

Krumdick, Victor F., and Lumian, Norman C. "The Psychology of Athletic Success." *Athletic Journal,* vol. 44, no. 1 (Sept. 1963), p. 52.

Kubistant, Tom. *Performing Your Best*. Champaign, Ill.: Human Kinetics, 1986.

Leonard, George. *The Ultimate Athlete*. New York: Viking Press, 1975.
    This book deals with a very zen and aikido-like perception and rethinking of the whole issue of contest and adversary. It is a very interesting and thoughtful book to help the sports enthusiast probe into the more complex dimensions of athletic performance.

Loudis, Leonard. *Skiing Out of Your Mind*. Champaign, Ill.: Human Kinetics, 1986.

Martens, Rainer. *Sport Competition Anxiety Test.* Champaign, Ill.: Human Kinetics, 1977.

Michener, James A. *Sports in America.* New York: Fawcett, 1976.
   This best book of its kind deals with the social and economic underpinnings of organized sports in the United States, and how sports affect all those involved.

Millman, Dan. *The Warrior Athlete.* Walpole, N.H.: Stillpoint Publishing, 1979.

Morgan, William, ed. *Contemporary Readings in Sport Psychology.* Springfield, Ill.: Charles C. Thomas Publishing, 1970.
   This is a very unusual edition by a variety of psychologists and scientists dealing with many aspects of sport performance ranging from the physiology of stress and performance to the psychological issues involved in motivation.

Morgan, William. "Selected Psychological Considerations in Sport." *Research Quarterly,* vol. 45 (Dec. 1974), pp. 374–390.

Murphy, Michael. *Gold in the Kingdom.* New York: Viking Press, 1972.
   This is an interesting, though somewhat tongue-in-cheek, attempt to attune the athlete to mental and spiritual abilities that each of us carries within him. The scene is set in Scotland where an old mystic golf pro teaches the rational American a whole new approach to golf.

Murphy, M., and White, Rhea. *The Psychic Side of Sports.* Menlo Park, Calif.: Addison Wesley, 1978.
   Psychic and transpersonal dimensions of sports are addressed. This is a very comprehensive book and the best introductory book of its kind. It has an extensive bibliography, which is its best feature. The book is excellent, but very difficult to apply.

Naruse, Gosaku. "The Hypnotic Treatment of Stage Fright in Champion Athletes." *International Journal of Clinical and Experimental Hypnosis,* vol. 13 (Jan. 1965), pp. 63–70.

Neal, Patsy. *Sport and Identity.* Philadelphia: Dorrance, 1972.

Nicholi, Armand. "Psychiatric Considerations in Professional Football." *New England Journal of Medicine,* vol. 316, no. 17.
Contemporary article; applies aspects of sports psychology to professional football.

Nideffer, R. *The Ethics and Practice of Applied Sport Psychology.* Ithaca, N.Y.: Movement Publications, 1981.

_____. *Guide to Mental Training.* Champaign, Ill.: Human Kinetics, 1985.

_____. *The Inner Athlete.* New York: Thomas Crowell, 1976.
An excellent book that focuses on what an athlete does internally to facilitate or impede optimal performance. It also examines sports within a context of the deeper and more profound mental and emotional capacities of the human being.

Ogilvie, B., and Howe, R. "Beating the Slumps at Their Own Game." *Psychology Today,* July 1984, pp. 28–32.

Orlick, Terry. *Coaches' Training Manual to Psyching for Sport.* Champaign, Ill.: Human Kinetics, 1986.

_____. *In Pursuit of Excellence.* Champaign, Ill.: Human Kinetics, 1986.

_____. *Psyching for Sport.* Champaign, Ill.: Human Kinetics, 1986.

Pargman, David. *Stress and Motor Performance: Understanding and Coping.* Ithaca, N.Y.: Movement Publications, 1986.

Roberts, Glyn. *Learning Experiences in Sports Psychology.* Champaign, Ill.: Human Kinetics, 1981.

Robinson, J.G. *Reaching Your Athletic Potential.* Tigord, Ore.: Quality Publications, 1981.
This is an excellent, comprehensive book dealing with the mental dimensions of sports, all the way from training to performance and from goal setting to actualization. Covers all major areas. The only shortcoming is that it is a bit anecdotal and doesn't get to underlying structures or dynamics.

Ryan, Frank. *Sports and Psychology*. Englewood Cliffs, N.J.: Prentice Hall, 1981.
   A nontechnical book that addresses many of the human components of athletics.

Sacks, Michael. *Psychology of Running*. Champaign, Ill.: Human Kinetics, 1981.

Salmela, John. *World Sport Psychology Handbook*. Ithaca, N.Y.: Movement Publications, 1981.

Silwa, J., and Steinberg, R., eds. *Psychological Foundations of Sports*. Champaign, Ill.: Human Kinetics Publishers, 1984.
   This is a compendium of many authors. It is comprehensive in its scope, very insightful, but heavy on the academic slant. It does not get to the human side of sports and is more for academicians. Extensive footnotes, scholarly in scope, but very good overall.

Singer, Robert. *Peak Performance*. Ithaca, N.Y.: Movement Publications, 1986.

_____. *Sustaining Motivation in Sport*. Ithaca, N.Y.: Movement Publications, 1984.

Straub, William. *Sport Psychology: Analysis of Athlete Behavior*. Ithaca, N.Y.: Movement Publications, 1980.

Tutko, T., and Richards, J. *The Psychology of Coaching*. Boston: Allyn and Bacon, 1971.
   This is a fine book dealing with several crucial issues that a coach must be aware of and deal with in regard to his players' psyche, emotions and interpersonal interactions.

Vanek, Miraslav, and Cratty, Bryant. *Psychology of the Superior Athlete*. London: Macmillan, 1970.
   This is an excellent book, speaking to the applied clinical approach and dimensions of sports psychology. It has a very good bibliography and case histories, alerting readers to what is being done worldwide in sports psychology.

Warren, William. *Coaching and Motivation*. Englewood Cliffs, N.J.: Prentice Hall, 1983.
This book is a good overview of issues a coach should be competent in when working with his players. Several important themes are addressed, but not in much depth and not necessarily from a psychological perspective.

Index

DATE DUE		